D1043769

BALE

MATT AND TOM OLDFIELD

ULTIMATE
FOOTBALL HEROES

BALE

FROM THE PLAYGROUND
TO THE PITCH

DINO

Published by Dino Books,
an imprint of John Blake Publishing,
2.25, The Plaza,
535 Kings Road,
Chelsea Harbour,
London SW10 0SZ

www.johnblakebooks.co.uk

www.facebook.com/johnblakebooks 🔳
twitter.com/jblakebooks 🔳

This edition published in 2015

ISBN: 978 1 78606 801 9

British Library Cataloguing-in-Publication Data:

A catalogue record for this book is available from the British Library.

Design by www.envydesign.co.uk

Printed and bound in Great Britain by Clays Ltd, Elcograf S.p.A.

7 9 10 8 6

© Text copyright Matt and Tom Oldfield 2017

Papers used by John Blake Publishing are natural, recyclable products made from wood grown in sustainable forests. The manufacturing processes conform to the environmental regulations of the country of origin.

Every reasonable effort has been made to trace copyright-holders of material reproduced in this book, but if any have been inadvertently overlooked the publishers would be glad to hear from them.

John Blake Publishing is an imprint of Bonnier Books UK
www.bonnierbooks.co.uk

To Mum and Dad

For all those mornings and afternoons on the

touchline, and for making all of this possible.

Matt Oldfield is an accomplished writer and the editor-in-chief
of football review site Of Pitch & Page. Tom Oldfield is a freelance
sports writer and the author of biographies on Cristiano Ronaldo,
Arsène Wenger and Rafael Nadal.

Cover illustration by Dan Leydon.
To learn more about Dan visit danleydon.com
To purchase his artwork visit etsy.com/shop/footynews
Or just follow him on Twitter @danleydon

TABLE OF CONTENTS

ACKNOWLEDGEMENTS

This was a very special opportunity for us, as brothers, to work together on something we are both so passionate about. Football has always been a big part of our lives. We hope this book will inspire others to start/continue playing football and chasing their dreams.

Writing a book like this was one of our dreams, and we are extremely thankful to John Blake Publishing and James Hodgkinson, in particular, for making this project possible.

We are also grateful to all the friends and family that encouraged us along the way. Your interest and sense of humour helped to keep us on track. Will, Doug, Mills, John, James Pang-Oldfield and the rest of our King Edward VI friends, our aunts, uncles, cousins, the Nottingham and Montreal families and so many others – thank you all.

Melissa, we could not have done this without your understanding and support. Thank you for being as excited about this collaboration as we were.

Noah, we're already doing our best to make football your favourite sport! We look forward to reading this book with you in the years ahead.

Mum and Dad, the biggest thank you is reserved for you. You introduced us to football and then devoted hours and hours to taking us to games. You bought the tickets, the kits, the boots. We love football because you encouraged us to. Thank you for all the love, all the laughs and for always believing in us. This book is for you.

CHAPTER 1

THE NEW GALÁCTICO

'*El nuevo jugador de Real Madrid, Gareth Bale.*'

'Real Madrid's new player, Gareth Bale.' When they called out his name, the stadium went wild. Thousands of fans clapped and cheered their new record signing. '*Bale! Bale! Bale!*' They chanted his name, the name that many of them already had on their shirts. Gareth couldn't believe it – this wasn't even his debut. He wasn't out there flying down the wing; he was wearing a suit. He could only guess how amazing the atmosphere would be for a game. As he got to his feet and walked up to the stage, he took a long, deep breath and told himself to stay calm. He was no longer the shy boy he once was, but he wasn't yet used to this kind of attention.

But even the butterflies in his stomach couldn't stop the big smile on Gareth's face. This was it; the biggest club in the world and the home of the *Galácticos*, the biggest superstars in the world. Luis Figo, Ronaldo, Raul, David Beckham, Cristiano Ronaldo... and now Gareth Bale. As a child, he'd sat with his father in the stands at his local ground Ninian Park watching his Uncle Chris play, pretending that it was the Bernabéu Stadium and that the Cardiff City team was the mighty Real Madrid. Now he was living out that fantasy and this time it was Gareth, not his uncle, who was the star.

As he approached the microphone, Gareth waved to the fans and then to his loved ones. It meant the world to him that they were all here for his big day: his mother Debbie and his father Frank, his grandad Dennis, his older sister Vicky, his best friend Ellis and, of course, his girlfriend Emma and their beautiful young daughter Alba. Without their endless support, he knew he would never have made it here.

When things settled down a bit, Gareth began: *'Es un sueño para mi jugar para Real Madrid. Gracias por esta gran acogida. ¡Hala Madrid!'* These were the first Spanish words he'd learnt and, of course, the most important. He'd practised them for days so that even in the excitement, he wouldn't forget them: 'It's my dream to play for Real Madrid. Thank you for this big welcome. Come on, Madrid!' The noise was incredible, so loud that he'd had to pause halfway through.

And then came the moment everyone had been waiting for, especially Gareth. He'd imagined it so many times but this time it was real. The President of Real Madrid held up the famous white shirt and there was his name in big black letters across the back: 'BALE'. The cameras flashed and the crowd roared once more. He was a *Galáctico* now – the most expensive of them all – and so his old number 3 shirt was no longer good enough. As he had in his last season at Tottenham, now he wore number 11, the number of his childhood hero, the Manchester United wing wizard Ryan Giggs.

Michael Owen had worn number 11 at Real Madrid in 2004, as had Arjen Robben in 2007. Gareth was proud to follow in their footsteps but he was determined to make that shirt his own. Watching the scenes around him, Gareth couldn't wait for the biggest challenge of his life. He was the most expensive player in the world and there would be a lot of pressure on him to join his teammate Cristiano Ronaldo as one of the very best players of all time.

As he did keepie-uppies on the Bernabéu pitch, Gareth thought back to his childhood days at Caedelyn Park. As a lightning-fast teenager in Wales, his family and coaches had predicted big things for him but no one had predicted this. At both Southampton and Tottenham, there had been difficult times when injuries looked like they might end Gareth's childhood dream. But the Welsh dragon had battled on and made it to the top.

CHAPTER 2

UNCLE CHRIS, CARDIFF CITY HERO

Gareth had hardly slept but he wasn't tired. He'd never been so excited. Today, on this autumn day in 1992, and for the first time in his life, he was off to watch his Uncle Chris – Chris Pike – play for Cardiff City. He'd seen him score a goal on the television once but never live at Ninian Park with thousands of other fans. Now that he was three, his dad, Frank, had decided that he was finally old enough to go to a game.

Gareth couldn't wait. The morning went so slowly as he watched the clock, and he begged it to fast-forward to 3 pm. To help the time pass, he made his sister stand in goal in the hallway and he took shots like his uncle. Vicky wasn't a very good keeper and the soft football kept whizzing past her. *GOAL! GOAL! GOAL! The crowd goes wild!* Finally at 1.45, Gareth stood ready at the front door, wearing the blue Cardiff City shirt and blue-and-white scarf that his uncle had given him for Christmas.

'Gareth, on the way to the ground you mustn't let go of your dad's hand,' his mum, Debbie, told him as she zipped up his coat and put gloves in the pockets. 'There'll be a lot of people there and you could easily get lost and miss the match. Now you don't want that, do you? So promise me, you won't let go of your dad's hand.'

'I promise, Mum!' But Gareth wasn't really listening to his worried mother. He was thinking about the football match and how many goals Uncle Chris would score. He was Cardiff's superstar striker, their top goalscorer for three years in a row, Gareth's dad had told him. If he was lucky, maybe Uncle Chris would score a hat-trick for him.

To get to Ninian Park, they had to take the train, which was an adventure in itself for a young child. They arrived at the local station in plenty of time to see the single carriage pull slowly up to the platform. Soon they were off, past the gate across the tracks that they used to get to Caedelyn Park. Then from the quiet, green spaces of Whitchurch they made their way towards the noisy, crowded city centre. Gareth stared out of the window as the view shifted from nice gardens to big, ugly buildings.

'Dad, how many times have you been to see Cardiff play? Five? Ten? A hundred?' he asked when he got bored of the view.

Frank laughed at the jump in numbers. 'I'm not sure, son, but it must be close to a hundred by now. I was going to watch the Bluebirds long before your uncle started playing for them... long before you were even born!'

At each stop on the route, the train got busier

and busier, and louder and louder. By Cardiff
Central station, fans were practising their chants
and talking about the team's best tactics. There
were many players that they didn't like but they
all seemed to love Uncle Chris. From Ninian
Park Station, it was a short walk to the ground
but it took a long time because the streets were
so busy.

The experience was even better than he'd hoped.
Still holding his father's hand, Gareth went through
the blue turnstiles, then up the blue steps to his blue
seat. The pitch looked so big and the players looked
so small as they warmed up below. He tried to find
his uncle. There he was in the penalty area, taking
shots at the goalkeeper. Gareth waved and waved but
of course his uncle didn't see him. He was focused
on the game, plus there were thousands of faces in
the crowd.

As the game kicked off, the noise was incredible.
The Cardiff City fans never stopped singing for their
team. Gareth didn't know many of the words but
he joined in with the clapping and the shouts of

'Come on, Cardiff!' He'd have to ask his father to teach him the songs later. After twenty minutes, a Cardiff defender played a long pass and suddenly Uncle Chris was through on goal. The fans started to rise from their seats, calling for him to score... but the goalkeeper ran out and made a good save to deny him. At half-time, the score was still 0-0 and his father was looking nervous next to him. But why? Gareth was sure that Uncle Chris would score a goal and win the match for them.

And he did. With time running out, the Cardiff winger dribbled down the right and crossed the ball high into the penalty area. Gareth followed the ball as it floated, as if in slow motion, through the air and on to the head of... Uncle Chris! He had jumped higher than the defender and the ball flew past the goalkeeper and into the top corner of the net. 1-0!

His uncle ran towards the Cardiff supporters to celebrate, waving his fists with joy. In the excitement, everyone was up on their feet and for a moment, Gareth couldn't see a thing. He tugged on his father's sleeve and Frank lifted his son on to his shoulders to get a better view. From up high, Gareth cheered and cheered until his throat was sore. 'That's my uncle!' he told the fans around him. It was the greatest feeling in the world.

The game ended 1-0 and as they walked home, Gareth asked his father if they could go to the next game.

'Yes, if you behave yourself,' Frank replied with a grin, and took out the fixture list. 'Right, Cardiff are playing away at Bury next Saturday but the weekend after that, it'll be Gillingham at home.'

Two weeks?! He had to wait fourteen whole days?! It seemed like a lifetime. Oh well, if he couldn't watch football every day, he would play it every day, and if he played it every day, he'd get better and better until he became as good as his uncle. Or maybe even better.

When they got home, his mother opened the front door. 'Did you enjoy the game, son?' she asked, helping him out of his coat.

But it was a pointless question; she already knew

the answer because Gareth was smiling so much. 'Mum, it was amazing! We won 1-0 and Uncle Chris scored! When I grow up, I'm going to be a footballer just like him! Dad, can we go to the park tomorrow to practise?'

CHAPTER 3

GIGGSY IN THE GARDEN

'Giggsy's on the run, past one defender, then another… and another! What an incredible run this is! He's through on goal with just the keeper to beat. From twenty yards out, he aims for the bottom corner… What a goooooaaaaaaaallllll!'

Gareth turned away to celebrate, his Cardiff City shirt lifted high up over his head, his arms outstretched like an aeroplane. To complete his routine, he did 'The Klinsmann', throwing him-self down onto the grass, arms stretched out in front of him like he was diving into a swimming pool. His mum would be furious – more football kit covered in mud and grass stains. His friend

Ellis had hardly moved in goal. It wasn't as much fun without real defenders but a goal was still a goal.

The aspiring footballer had been working hard on his shooting after school on his own, in the dark and often in the rain, hitting the ball as hard as he could at targets that he placed around the garden. It took time for him to find his accuracy, as a quick look next-door would show. Every day, Mr Tout would throw the footballs back over the fence but Gareth was too shy to knock on his door and ask for them. When he kicked one over, he'd hear his neighbour mutter and curse. The best Gareth could do was shout a quick 'Sorry!' and then run back into the house.

His parents weren't too happy either about the damage to their plants, but it was better than Gareth playing in the house. 'Gareth, go outside for a bit,' his father would say when he saw him fighting with his sister over what TV channel to watch. 'You've got too much energy.' Like a puppy, Gareth needed his exercise. Both of his parents were big sports fans and it was hard for them to complain about their son showing such an interest in something. But that didn't stop Debbie from wishing that Gareth cared as much about his times tables.

Gareth wasn't the worst student but he wasn't the best either. Like a lot of other seven-year-old boys, he was clever and did well when he tried hard, but there was usually something else on his mind. When he wasn't playing football, he was normally dreaming about it, or thinking about it. How would it feel to score the winning goal in a cup final? What would he need to do to become the best? He knew he was faster than the other kids he played against for Eglwys Newydd Primary School, but he had to work on his other skills like passing, dribbling, tackling and heading.

There was a long way to go if he was going to be as good as his new hero, Ryan Giggs. The Manchester United wizard was taking the Premier League by storm, making defenders look silly with his amazing abilities. Gareth loved watching him with the ball at his feet, moving one way and then the other – it was so exciting. 'That kid's got everything,' Gareth's father said one day when they watched Giggs on TV. 'In a year or two, he'll be one of the best in the world.' Gareth was sixteen years younger but they had three things in common: they were both Welsh, they were both left-footed wingers and they were both really fast. Anything was possible.

That was Gareth's dream, even at the age of six – to play against the best teams in the world and win lots of trophies. 'Practice makes perfect,' his other hero, Uncle Chris, would say as Gareth tried to dribble past him for the hundredth time. 'You were almost there that time – try it again. Remember, make your decision early and don't stop.' Come rain or shine, Gareth never gave up until he succeeded, even when he was out of breath, his face was red and sweaty, and his legs were heavy and painful. Even his mum calling him in for dinner couldn't stop Gareth. When it came to sport, he never ran out of energy.

Thank goodness, because Gareth was already in high demand. In Wales, rugby would always be the number one sport. At Caedelyn Park, for example, there were eight sets of rugby posts and only four football goals, although sometimes they'd use the space under the posts as a goal. The rugby coaches thought Gareth could be a great winger, even if he was a bit small and skinny for such a tough game. He was a good kicker and, of course, he had the speed to run the length of the pitch to score lots of tries.

Gareth wanted to play as many sports as possible, as often as possible, but his heart lay with football. He was just much more comfortable with a ball at his feet than he was with it in his hands. Frank, who had played both football and rugby as a boy, was very happy to let Gareth decide for himself. 'Son, I'll support you in whichever sport you choose to play. Unless it's ballet!'

For now, though, football in the garden was the main focus. 'Right, my turn!' his best friend Ellis shouted as he reached carefully into the rose bush to get the ball back. He hardly ever saved Gareth's shots; they were too powerful and accurate. Placing the ball down on the edge of the grass, Ellis began his commentary. 'Jamie Redknapp has the ball in midfield for Liverpool. He spots Robbie Fowler's run and plays a perfect pass. Fowler beats the centre- back with ease and he's through on goal! The keeper comes out... but he can't stop that. Gooooooooaaaaaaaaalllllllllllllll!'

As Ellis kissed the ground with delight, Gareth hit the ground with anger. Even messing about in his own back garden, he hated to lose. He should have saved it but only his fingertips could make contact with the ball. He'd had enough of this kick-about – he wanted to play a proper match on a proper pitch with proper opponents. He wanted to have the space to run at defenders and score goals.

It was half-term and there was still a whole afternoon to play. It was perfect weather for football – not too hot, not too cold, no wind and no rain. Gareth picked up the ball and walked towards the

gate. 'Shall we go and see if there's anyone down at
the park? As long as we're back before it gets dark,
my mum won't mind.'

CHAPTER 4

SCOUTED

Stuck in Bank Holiday traffic on the Severn Bridge going across to Wales, Rod was very tempted to turn around and go home. The weather was nice and he could have been sitting outside with the newspaper and a good book, perhaps doing a bit of gardening if he felt like it. Instead, he was sitting in a hot car that wasn't moving, and he was late for an Under-9s six-a-side football tournament in Newport. The chances of finding a young talent at these things was so small but the fear of missing the 'next big thing' kept him going year after year.

'There are a lot of good young kids playing in Wales at the moment,' his boss at Southampton Football

Club had told him on the phone a few days before. 'Go and have a look and see if anyone catches your eye.' Rod had been scouting since 1985 and made these journeys all the time. It was very difficult to spot the eight-year-old who would still be a promising player at eighteen, and then develop into a great player in his twenties. Small boys sometimes suddenly grew tall and strong, and bigger boys sometimes stopped growing. Years of experience helped him make his selections, but he still often made mistakes.

When he finally arrived in Newport, Rod walked out onto the busy playing fields. There were six small pitches set out for sixteen teams, plus substitutes, coaches and families. Dog owners fought to keep their pets under control and the burger van was very busy by the car park. *'Paul, how did you miss that?!'* *'Danny, you've got to be stronger there!' 'Don't mess around with it back there, son!'* The air was filled with the shouts of parents on the touchline. Rod hated the pressure that some of them put on their children. 'At this age, they should just be enjoying football,' he said to himself.

After walking around all of the pitches, he stopped to watch a lad who was certainly enjoying his football. Over on the furthest pitch, a small, skinny left-footed player was giving the opposition a game to forget. Each time he got the ball deep in his own half, he attacked straight away and at an incredible pace. The pitches were narrow but that wasn't stopping him. Sometimes he dribbled past the defenders; other times he just kicked it ahead and ran past everyone to catch up with it. Either way, he never stopped running; he was at the centre of everything.

'What's the score here?' Rod asked the linesman, who was struggling with the speed of the game. Sweat dripped down his forehead.

'I've lost count already!' he replied. 'It's at least 10-nil and there are still five minutes to go.'

As he said this, the kid weaved his way through again and this time, rather than pass to a teammate, he shot powerfully into the bottom corner. The other players ran to celebrate with him but they couldn't keep up. So he could run and dribble, and he could shoot, too. 'This kid is impressive!' he thought to himself. 'Great play, Gareth!' he heard the Cardiff Civil Service coach shout. It was always good to put a name to a face.

At the end of the game, the boy shook hands with each of his opponents before jogging over to a group that Rod guessed was his parents, grandad and sister. He liked Gareth's behaviour: polite, modest and caring towards his family. For someone with such ability, he seemed almost shy about it. That was unusual and these were very important signals when looking for the best young players. Perhaps today would be more interesting than he'd expected.

'You can have all the talent in the world but if the attitude isn't right, there's a good chance it will all go wrong.' Rod had made that speech many times over the years. You needed confidence but you also needed a desire to work hard and keep improving.

It was still early days with Gareth. Often the kids that Rod watched would have one brilliant game and then go quiet in the next. Word would spread that a player was good, teams would mark him tightly, and he would struggle to find the room to do his normal tricks. He would have to wait and see if Gareth could do it again.

After half an hour, the kid was back out on the pitch. The way he warmed up, stretching his arms and shaking his legs, it was like he couldn't stay still. He certainly looked excited to be playing again; that was how it should be for these kids. The first few times he got the ball, a defender ran straight in and fouled him. Gareth picked himself up off the grass each time and never complained to the referee. As Rod had predicted, word had spread about Gareth. This was the big test now.

The fourth time he got the ball, he played a neat one-two with a teammate and suddenly he had what he was looking for – space. 'Great players create space out of nothing' – that was another of Rod's favourite lessons. 'Nice, quick feet' – Rod made another note in his head. In the blink of an eye, the young Welsh lad raced down the wing and crossed perfectly for the striker to tap the ball into the net – 1-0! This kid was in a different league to everyone else. The match ended 8-1, with Gareth getting a hat-trick of goals and a hat-trick of assists. And he didn't even look tired.

Rod watched with growing excitement as Gareth played the key role in game after game. Today was the kind of day that made his job feel so worthwhile. This was a special talent he was watching; he was sure this was a player they would want at the Southampton academy. Gareth had both the skill and the attitude that he was looking for. You had to move fast with these things – you never knew which other clubs had scouts at these tournaments – but it was also important to obey the rules. As the teams left the field, Rod walked along the touchline and introduced himself to the Cardiff Civil Service manager. Once he was happy that Rod was really a scout, the coach then introduced him to Gareth's father, Frank.

'Hello, it's very nice to meet you. My name's Rod and I'm a scout for Southampton Football Club. I understand the hat-trick hero is your kid?'

Frank nodded proudly. 'Yes, his name's Gareth. He's having a good day today – the whole team are.'

It was Rod's turn to nod. 'The kid's certainly got a lot of talent. Is he playing for a club yet?'

'Just for the local team and his school at the moment.'

'I'd really love for Gareth to visit our football academy in Bath, just for a few training sessions to see if he likes it. Here's my card – please have a think about my offer and give me a call if you're interested. Gareth seems like a very nice kid. I think you've got a fantastic player there.'

'Thanks, Rod. It was nice to meet you,' Frank said, taking the card and offering a handshake. The scout could tell where Gareth got his good manners from. 'I'll speak to my son and I'll speak to my wife, and I'll be in touch soon.'

CHAPTER 5

TRAINING WITH THE SAINTS

'Hello, Gareth,' Rod said with a big smile and a strong handshake. 'Welcome to the Southampton Football Club Satellite Centre! I'm really pleased that you could come and visit us.'

Gareth smiled back shyly, glad to have his dad by his side. He still couldn't believe it was really happening. Frank and Debbie had discussed Rod's invitation straight after the tournament, once their son had gone to bed with his 'tournament winner' and 'best player' medals still around his neck. His mum was worried that it could be a lot of pressure at such a young age. 'And as if he needs more of a distraction from his school work!' she warned her husband. In the end, however, they agreed that it should be Gareth's decision.

They told their son the next day after school and it was the happiest moment of his life so far. Gareth jumped up off the sofa and danced around the living room.

'That's the best news ever – Southampton want me to come and train with them! Please Mum and Dad, I really want to go! What if I never get another offer? It's not too far away and I promise I will work extra hard at school.'

He begged and begged but he didn't really need to – Frank was just as excited as him. Once his parents had said yes, Gareth phoned his grandad Dennis and then went round to tell Ellis the amazing news. He was going to train with a top football academy! The next day, he was the talk of the school playground – '*Have you heard? Gareth's going to play in the Premier League!*', '*Yeah, apparently Manchester United want him too. And Arsenal...*' It was the kind of attention that he'd have to get used to one day.

On the hour-and-a-half car journey to Bath, there was little conversation. For the first time ever, Frank could tell that his son was nervous. He waited until they arrived before giving him a quick hug and saying, 'There's nothing to worry about, Gareth. Just do your best and enjoy it. That's the most important thing, son – have fun!' It was good to hear that from his dad, who always knew what to say to make him feel better.

The academy centre felt very large and professional. Rod took them on a tour of the changing rooms, the gym, the brand new training pitches. It was a long way from the local parks and playing fields where he normally played. Gareth had imagined that only the best players trained in places like this, but there were five-year-olds training here. They stopped to watch some of the Under-7s session, and the standard was very good. If even kids this young played nice passing football, what would the nine-year-olds be like? Gareth knew he was good but this was a much higher level than he'd ever played before. He just hoped he wouldn't let himself down.

'Can you see yourself enjoying it here, Gareth?' Rod asked at the end. Gareth nodded back eagerly and they all laughed. 'If you join us permanently, you'll get to go to the training ground in Southampton every week. It's even better!' Gareth couldn't imagine that but he didn't need persuading. All the kids had Southampton Football Club tracksuits and smart red training tops – he really hoped that he'd get the same kit to take home.

It was time to get ready for practice. The other nine-year-old boys had arrived and Rod introduced him to the group. He was definitely one of the smallest – some of them looked about fifteen! As they went in to get changed, the scout handed Gareth a red training top. 'This is yours now – welcome to Southampton Football Club!' He'd never seen the club badge up close before; a flower, water, and a tree, then a football with a halo on top of a scarf. How weird, he thought. Not that he cared, though – he would have worn anything.

Steven, the coach, was friendly and patient as he showed Gareth the training drills. He was the only new player, and all the other boys looked like they'd been doing it for years. After a long, hard warm-up, they did some passing exercises, moving the ball quickly to keep hold of it. The technique of all the kids was really good and they hardly ever made mistakes, but Gareth felt like he was holding his own pretty well. Just wait until they saw him speeding up the wing.

During a short rest, he looked up and saw his dad and Rod watching. His father waved, but Gareth was too embarrassed to wave back. The other kids seemed nice, but he didn't want them to think he was a daddy's boy.

After an hour, Steven divided the boys into two teams of eight and they played a match. This was what Gareth had been waiting for – the chance to really impress. This wasn't local Cardiff football anymore, however. The defenders were bigger, stronger and faster, and they weren't going to let the new kid get the better of them. Gareth managed to score one near the end but overall, he wasn't very pleased with his performance. Had he done enough to be invited back again?

When Steven blew the final whistle, the other boys jogged in to shower and get changed, with their parents waiting impatiently in their cars. But Gareth wasn't finished yet. He placed six balls across the edge of the penalty area. One by one he hit them, aiming for different areas of the goal. A couple went wide, but most found the net. Then he did it all over again. Power and accuracy – that's what he needed.

'Come on Gareth, we've got to go now!' his dad called from the touchline. 'You've got school tomorrow, kiddo!'

As Gareth finally walked off the pitch, Rod ruffled his hair. 'Good work today, lad. That's some work-rate you've got there. Steven was impressed – he'd like you to come back next week, if that's okay with you?'

In a second, Gareth's frown was turned upside

down. 'Yes please!' he replied. He was so relieved
to get another chance. Next time, he'd be so much
better.

CHAPTER 6

PLAYTIME

'Big ears, you can pick first!' Ellis shouted, throwing Gareth the ball. 'I'm feeling lucky today – I think my team might win for once!'

'OK, but I wouldn't get too hopeful if I was you,' Gareth replied with a cheeky smile. He did a few keepie-uppies and balanced the ball on the back of his neck. 'It's not luck you need – it's talent!'

It was lunchtime and fourteen boys were lined up on the tarmacked playground at Eglwys Newydd Primary. It was a normal late winter's day, with the sun trying to warm things up a little. Football did a better job of warming them up, though, and they quickly took their school jumpers off once play

began. Now that they were the oldest kids in the
school as well as the best players, Gareth and Ellis
got to be the team captains.

Every day, they picked their soldiers and went
into battle – it was easily their favourite thing about
school! Fifteen minutes before the lunch bell, the
excitement would start to build. For that quarter of
an hour, their eyes never left the classroom clock.
They kept score in the back of their exercise books –
Gareth 41 wins, Ellis 12. The teams were normally
pretty fair but having a Southampton academy player
always made a difference.

Ellis was the only one who got away with teasing
Gareth; if anyone else made fun of him, they were
quickly punished with an embarrassing football
lesson. Off the sports field, he was still shy and polite
but on it, Gareth was the opposite. There was a
fire inside him that only got started when he had
a ball and a goal. This pitch was very small – there
was a wet-weather shelter on one touchline and a
hopscotch painted along the other – but that never
stopped him. In fact, Gareth loved the challenge; the

less space he had, the better his technique needed to be in order to win. He was a natural athlete with a real competitive streak, and so he hardly ever lost.

'Come on, we haven't got all day. You're not playing for Southampton Football Club now, you know!'

Ellis had decided that it was his job to keep his best friend's feet firmly on the ground, especially now that he was travelling to Bath for training every week as well as playing matches for the club every Sunday. Gareth had even met Saints legend Matt Le Tissier! Despite all this, however, Ellis's job wasn't very difficult. Gareth very rarely boasted. He knew how lucky he was and let his skills do the talking instead. 'Everyone's really nice and they're making me a better player,' was all Gareth would say when his friends asked him about the Southampton sessions.

Yes, he was definitely getting better. He was still small for his age but he was getting stronger and the academy coaching was really improving his instincts. Steven was always urging him to think more and to read the game better. 'If you can see more of what's going on around you,' he told Gareth, showing a full circle of vision with his hands, 'you'll make better decisions, and decisions win matches.'

With this added power, Gareth was also getting even faster. With Rod watching, he finished second in the Welsh Schools Under-11s 50m sprint. He hadn't expected to do so well but to get so close was painful – he hated to lose. 'I started too slowly – I only gave myself the last twenty metres to catch him up. Never enough time,' he panted at the finish line. 'Don't beat yourself up about it, Gareth,' his dad said, patting him on the back. 'You were brilliant and there's always the Under-12s, the Under-13s, the Under-14s...' He stopped there because he knew it wasn't working – Gareth didn't say a word on the journey home and left his silver medal in the car. If it wasn't gold, he didn't really want it.

Back at Eglwys Newydd Primary, the teams had been picked and it was time to toss a coin for kick-off and ends. It was best to shoot towards the High School because the fence was a bit higher than the one leading out onto the street. These things really mattered.

Ellis's team talk was brief and always the same: 'Ryan and Johnny – your job is to watch Gareth. Follow him everywhere and give him a bit of a shove when you need to.'

Gareth's, on the other hand, was more detailed: 'Scott and Dunc, you're the defence – don't get drawn too far forward and stick to your men. We know they're going to mark me tightly, so there'll be space for you guys. Danny, Mark, Sam, get into good positions and I'll find you. Let's win this!'

The game was played at a really fast pace. The lunch hour always flew by so fast and there wasn't a minute to waste. Gareth scored eight and set up most of the others as they won 23-9. It was a good victory and very much a team victory. 'Until next time!' Ellis joked as they shook hands at the end. Sometimes they even swapped jumpers.

The teachers called them all inside and they made their way back to the classroom, red-faced, sweaty and exhausted. There hadn't been any injuries but parents would have yet more sewing to do to patch up trousers. All the talk was about the lunchtime game: who had played well and who hadn't, who had scored the best goal. It was always an impossible job to get them to concentrate on science first thing in the afternoon.

Before he went inside, Gareth took one last look over the fence at Whitchurch High School in the distance with its big playing fields and Astroturf pitches. He'd be going there next year and he couldn't wait. It would be a shock to go from the top of one school to the bottom of another, but he was ready. They had one of the best football teams in Wales and he was determined to be their new star player.

CHAPTER 7

PRACTICE
MAKES PERFECT

Secondary school was everything Gareth hoped
it would be: sport, sport and more sport. Rugby,
hockey, running and, of course, football – he played
them all and he did well at each. He scored in a
Welsh schools hockey final and he ran the 100
metres in just 11.4 seconds! 'Is there any sport you
can't play?' the headmaster joked with him one
day. Rather than hold him back, the Southampton
academy had told him to play as many different
sports as he wanted. Perhaps they hoped that
rugby would toughen him up. But despite his great
performances at full back, he decided that it wasn't
for him.

'Dad, I'm thinking about giving up rugby,' Gareth said suddenly one evening at the dinner table, his head bent over a plate of spaghetti bolognese. He had wanted to say something for weeks but it was difficult when his dad was such a big fan of the Welsh national sport. His mum and sister stopped their conversation to listen. 'I'm too skinny for such a physical sport. Look at the rest of the team – they're so much bigger than me! Every tackle hurts for days and I'm worried that one of these days I'll get a bad injury, and then what about Southampton?'

Slowly he looked up to see his dad's reaction. He expected him to be disappointed but Frank was nodding. 'Gareth, I think you're right but I wanted you to make that decision for yourself. It's so stressful watching you racing down that rugby field; it's like watching a flimsy branch creaking in a strong wind. I fear you're going to get snapped in half at any moment!' They all laughed at this image, including Gareth. What a relief that his dad wasn't angry. So they all agreed – it was time to really focus on his football career.

The school weren't pleased but they allowed Gareth a free pass to skip rugby, just as they allowed him to take days off to travel to Southampton and back on his own, as long as he caught up with his schoolwork. His mates understood too but that didn't stop them from teasing him for months.

'Gareth, it's raining – do you need me to get you an umbrella? We can't have you getting wet and ruining your football career.'

'Be careful lifting that bag, Gareth! Think of the back problems that could cause a skinny lad like you…'

The PE teacher was just as tough with him. Gwyn pushed Gareth harder than the others, telling him to look up earlier and be more physical. 'Get those hands dirty!' was the phrase that Gareth hated most. Now that he was putting football first, he had to give it his all. One day, as Gwyn picked the teams for a match at the end of a football session, he decided to introduce a new rule.

'Gareth, we all know how good that left foot of yours is, but what about the right? Can you use it, or is it just for balance? Well, we're about to find out because in this game, you're only allowed to use your right foot. If I see you touch it with your left, I'll give a free kick to the opposition!'

Some of his teammates looked shocked but Gareth just shrugged and jogged out onto the pitch. He wasn't going to complain, even if it was like taking away a superhero's super power. He knew Gwyn was just trying to make him a better player, and that's what he wanted too. He wasn't all that confident on his right foot yet but he'd been practising for months. 'We don't want to hear about a weaker foot,' the Southampton coaches had told the Under-14s squad at the start of the season. 'There should be no such thing at this level. We're looking for all-round players, not one-trick ponies.'

'I guess it's time to test my progress,' Gareth thought positively as the game kicked off. It was harder than it looked, though. Under pressure from a defender, he shifted the ball from right to left. Gwyn blew the whistle straight away. 'Free kick to the blues!' Gareth kicked the air in frustration. It felt so unnatural but it got easier with each touch. Soon, he was making good passes.

'That's it Gareth – your standing leg's not so bad after all!' Gwyn encouraged him from the touchline. Gareth smiled back but said under his breath, 'Right, now I'll show you what my right foot can do!'

He got the ball on the edge of the penalty area and with his first touch, he wrong-footed the defender who had expected him to go left as normal. Then with his second touch, he sent a fierce strike low into the bottom corner. His teammates ran over to celebrate with him and some even kissed the goalscoring boot.

After the game, Gareth went over to shake Gwyn's hand. 'Thanks for the challenge,' he said with a cheeky grin on his face.

'My pleasure, you did very well,' the PE teacher replied. 'Now you've got to keep it up. Maybe we'll make that rule a permanent thing!'

CHAPTER 8

NERVOUS TIMES

'Good news – I've got trials at Cardiff City next week,' Sam blurted out as they walked down the long driveway to their school. It was a cold autumn morning and they kicked the golden leaves that covered the path. Sam was so excited that he just couldn't keep it a secret any longer. He knew that Gareth of all his friends would understand. He'd wanted to tell him before Ellis and the others arrived.

'That's brilliant – congrats mate!' Gareth replied, giving him a quick hug. He was so pleased that a close friend and teammate was following in his footsteps. Sam was a big, powerful centre-back, good in the air and also quick on his feet. As one of the stars of the school rugby team too, he was another natural, all-round athlete like Gareth. Whitchurch High School seemed to have quite a few of them.

'Yes, I didn't really want to tell any of you guys in case it goes really badly,' he said quietly as they walked through the corridor to class. 'But in the end I couldn't help it! Any tips for the big day?' Sam was normally a confident person but he looked nervous already and he still had a whole week to go.

Having thought for a minute about his first few sessions at the academy in Bath, Gareth gave the best advice he could. 'Just keep it simple and play your normal game. Under pressure, you'll try to do fancy things to catch the eye. That's a bad idea – trust me!' Sam nodded to show he'd made a note of this.

Gareth was glad that he'd never had to go through a real trial at Southampton. Competing with a big group of other players at a one-off session seemed like such a tough process to go through. What if you were the best player there but had a bad day? It must happen all the time. At least he'd had several chances to impress.

'Also Sam, listen carefully to what the coaches ask you to do,' he added, thinking back to Rod's helpful guidance. 'They're looking for fast learners who really want to get better.'

'Cheers Gareth – I should be writing this stuff down!' Sam replied.

'No problem, mate. Most importantly, though, have fun! That's what Dad told me on my first day at Southampton.'

'I'll try to enjoy the experience, despite all of the nerves!'

Gareth was starting to feel the nerves more and more himself. Now that they were getting closer to that key 15–16 age group, each training session and each match felt like a trial. In the next year or two, Southampton Football Club had to make the big decisions about which of their youngsters would get scholarships, and which they would have to let go.

'Make or break' was how Gareth was seeing it, even if neither the coaching staff nor his family were calling it that. His parents and Vicky never stopped supporting him and travelled with him to Southampton twice a month to cheer him on. They could tell that Gareth was starting to get more stressed about his football. 'It's just another match,' his father would say to him before each game. 'Just go out there and show them what you've got!'

It wasn't his football skills that the Southampton coaches were worried about; it was his size. Gareth was still only five feet five inches and there was no sign of the growth spurt that was happening to all the other kids around him. There were players his age that were already over six feet tall! How could he compete against these giants? Each morning before school, he would ask his mother to measure him and mark it on the wall in pencil. The progress was very, very slow.

'Mum, Southampton are never going to give me a scholarship when I'm this small,' Gareth said one day, staring moodily into his bowl of cereal. 'What can I do to make myself taller?'

She hated to see her son so unhappy. 'Gareth, there's nothing you can do except wait for nature to take its course. Keep playing well and it will happen, I promise. You'll be six foot before you know it!'

Gareth nodded but he didn't believe her. His dad wasn't that tall and the coaches at Southampton had said that some players only stopped growing at nineteen – that was five whole years away. There was no way that he, or the club, could wait that long.

Thank goodness there was some good news in Gareth's life. Emma had agreed to go on a date with him. With her long brown hair and lovely smile, Gareth thought she was the most beautiful girl in the world. He had noticed her on the very first day of school. When he got to know her, he found that they laughed at the same things and were both very close to their families. Emma had two sisters, Katie and Charlotte, who were also her best friends. She liked to call herself a 'homebird', and Gareth really liked that about her.

'Gareth, will you please just ask Emma out?' Ellis said as they warmed up before football, rolling his eyes in frustration. 'It's getting boring now! Clearly she likes you and clearly you like her – what's the problem? Are you just too scared?'

Gareth shrugged and stayed quiet. He was still shy about these things – what if she said no? Not happy with his silence, Sam started making chicken noises and the rest of the team joined in. It went on for what felt like hours, until their coach arrived and told them to stop it. Gareth was very glad when the football started.

It took him months to pluck up the courage but then one day as they all left the football field, Emma came over to say hello. She looked so pretty and he looked awful: sweaty, muddy and red-faced! He felt embarrassed that she'd seen him like this. Ellis and Sam left them to it, but not before giving Gareth 'the look' – it was time for him to ask her. He took a deep breath to calm his nerves.

'Err, Emma would you… like to go to the cinema with me this weekend?' Gareth managed to ask after a few stumbles. He could hear the shaking in his voice. Phew, he had finally done it. Now he just had to wait for a response.

Emma smiled and blushed. 'I'd love to... but why did it take you so long to ask me? I thought I was going to have to ask you out but my sisters wouldn't let me do that!'

He was so happy and relieved. 'I guess I was scared that you might not want to,' he tried to explain but it sounded silly now. 'It's weird, I never get this nervous on the pitch!'

Emma laughed. 'You might be a born footballer, Gareth, but you're not a born romantic!'

CHAPTER 9

GROWING PAINS I

Things were going really well with Emma. She was so caring and supportive, and just when he most needed support too. The growth spurt had begun but it wasn't the great news that he had hoped it would be.

'Gareth, these pains are completely normal,' the Southampton physio told him one day at the Staplewood training ground. He prodded Gareth's lower back in various places, and the boy winced at the shooting pain from each touch. 'Your body is just getting used to the fact that you're getting taller. You need to stop playing for a couple of weeks and then we'll take another look.'

Gareth got up off the treatment table, thanked the physio and limped out. His dad was waiting for him outside and helped him into the car. 'What did he say?'

'I need to rest it. He said it's just growing pains,' Gareth replied.

'Hey, that's good news!' his dad said, but he could see that his son wasn't at all pleased. 'Cheer up, at least it's nothing serious.'

'I know but I need to be playing right now,' Gareth explained. Out of the window he watched the Under-16s training session going on without him. 'More and more of the coaches are coming to our games and practices. What if I keep growing but can't play for a year?'

'Son, you just can't rush these things. And besides, remember when you thought you'd never grow? Well, now you are!'

Gareth smiled but he wasn't convincing anyone, least of all his father.

Two weeks without football was really hard for Gareth, and he became a very grumpy teenager. At the weekend, Emma tried to take his mind off things by taking him to Cardiff Bay for lunch. Afterwards, they took the Waterbus to Penarth and strolled along the windy seafront in the sun.

'Emma, thanks for today,' Gareth said as they ate their ice creams on the pier. 'It's been a really nice day out and I'm sorry I'm not better company at the moment. I just can't stop thinking about the team playing on without me.'

Emma squeezed his hand. 'Gareth, I know you're worried but you'll be back out there in no time. They need you but if you start playing again too soon, you could make things worse. And I don't know if I could handle a whole year of you sulking like this!'

They laughed and he felt a little happier. He loved how sensible and wise his girlfriend was. That evening, they watched *The X Factor* with his family. Gareth was in a better mood and joked, 'Maybe I'll take up singing if football doesn't work out.'

'With all that gel in your hair, you could definitely be in a boyband!' his dad teased.

It was Emma's turn next. 'I take it you've never heard him sing then? If you had, you wouldn't be encouraging him!' Everyone laughed and Gareth threw a sofa cushion at her.

It turned out to be a frustrating stop-start time for Gareth. He began training again after a month but things were still not back to normal. His back felt all wrong and he found it difficult to run. His movement was like a robot at times. If he didn't have speed, what use would he be? Slowly, his stamina came back but his lightning pace was still not there. In the club's sprint tests he managed to finish third, but he was quite a long way behind his friend and rival, Theo Walcott.

Georges, one of the academy coaches, found him on his own in the changing room afterwards. He'd thrown his shirt and boots on the floor and was sitting there with his head in his hands. Georges smiled to himself; this kid was so determined to be the best. He went over and patted him on the back. 'Gareth, you came third! And on the Yo-Yo test you did nearly double what some of the players did. So why are you in here looking sad?'

'Six months ago, I would have got the same time as Theo. I've lost my speed!' Gareth replied with a face like he'd just received a lifetime detention. Georges had lost count of the number of times he'd heard youngsters say dramatic things like this. All he needed was a reality check.

He sat down next to Gareth on the bench. 'I've known you a long time and I know how much you want to succeed. That's great but you can't always be so hard on yourself. You've only just turned fifteen, you're still growing and your body is getting used to the changes. You did really well today.'

Gareth thought a lot about Georges' words. Patience might not have been one of his strong points, but determination certainly was. If he wasn't as quick, he'd just have to be twice as skilful. He worked harder than ever on his strength and technique.

'It really is make-or-break time now,' he admitted

to Emma one evening. 'Time is running out for me to show Southampton why they have to give me a scholarship.'

'Well, show them then!' she replied with a smile.

CHAPTER 10

THE BREAKTHROUGH

'Gareth, you'll be playing for the Under-18s against Norwich on Saturday,' Georges announced after a cold January training session. 'It's a big game for you – good luck!'

This was Gareth's big moment – the Southampton staff knew it, Gareth's family knew it and, most importantly, Gareth himself knew it. This was his big opportunity to shine and stop the club from letting him leave. After all of the back problems over the previous year, people had started to doubt him. The Wales Schools side had ignored him yet again. Rod and Georges still believed in him, but the Southampton directors were worried that Gareth was still too small and weak to make it as a professional footballer. His attitude was perfect, but his strength wasn't.

'Wow, I really can't mess this up!' He didn't think he'd said it out loud, but Theo replied, 'I know, every game is so important now.'

'Yes, but you're the star player! You'll be playing for the first team soon. For me, this is it – if I play badly, they won't give me a scholarship. If I play well, hopefully they will,' he told Theo as they jogged back to the changing room. It sounded so simple when he talked about it but now it was all about actions, not words. He had to prove he was tough enough to handle a higher level of football.

'We better both have the games of our lives then!' Theo joked, slapping his friend on the back.

Gareth's mum and dad made the long journey east to support him. It took them nearly five hours to reach the Norwich training ground but on this day, of all days, they needed to be there for their son. The whole family had their fingers crossed. Frank managed to get a quick word with him before the game started.

'How are you feeling?' he asked from the touchline. Gareth was doing his stretches and looked calm and focused.

'Good thanks – my back feels better than it has for ages,' he replied, practising a quick sprint. He still couldn't run quite as fast as he used to but he was getting closer every day.

'Brilliant. Look son, we all know it's a big day for you but whatever happens, we're all so proud of you. OK? So go out there and treat this like a cup final. Leave it all on the field – that's what they say, isn't it?'

Gareth smiled, nodded and then ran in for the team huddle. Frank watched his son go and knew it was going to be a good day.

As the match kicked off, Gareth took a long, deep breath. Boy was he ready for this! As he ran towards the ball, his nerves disappeared and so did the back pains. He felt amazing, like he could beat anyone. The first forty-five minutes were the best he'd ever played. He was strong in defence and attacked brilliantly down the left wing, again and again and again. He didn't stop running for a second.

It was a game to quickly forget for the Norwich defence – they just couldn't handle Gareth's speed and skill. It was like he was a seven-year-old again, dribbling past everyone at Caedelyn Park. He didn't manage to get a goal himself but he helped Theo to score. By half-time, Theo had a hat-trick. The game finished 5-1, a massive win for the Saints. Gareth felt tired but he was really happy with how well he'd played. He had done all he could to earn that scholarship. Theo might have taken the match ball but on the biggest day of his football career so far, Gareth had proved his doubters wrong.

'You were right, Theo,' Gareth shouted as they celebrated at the final whistle. 'That really *was* the game of our lives!'

It was as if they'd won a cup final. His parents rushed over to him afterwards. 'Well done, you were amazing! I'm so proud of you,' his mum said, hugging him with tears in her eyes.

'If they don't want you after that, then Southampton are crazy!' his dad told him.

Next to congratulate him was Georges, and then

Malcolm, the Southampton youth director, who
had come to the game to make his final decision.
'You played brilliantly today, Gareth,' Malcolm
said, shaking his hand. Hearing those words from
someone so important was the most amazing feeling.
'That was one of the best wing displays I've seen in
years. I bet that right-back is going to be seeing you
in his nightmares for a while!'

The youth director turned to speak to his parents.
'I think you can have a very happy trip back to
Wales. What a game! Your son's got a long future
here at Southampton Football Club.'

Gareth couldn't stop smiling at that news.

CHAPTER 11

MOVING ON

'And the winner of the PE department's prize for services to sport is...'

The Headmaster gave a long pause and pretended to look at his notes but everyone knew who the winner would be. The whole school was in the assembly hall for the end-of-school awards ceremony.

'... Gareth Bale!'

It was definitely the loudest response to any of the awards. What a great way to say goodbye to Whitchurch High. As Gareth made his way from his seat to the stage to collect his trophy, everyone clapped and cheered. *Gareth! Gareth! Gareth!* Ellis, Sam and his other pals were on their feet chanting his name and so were Emma and her friends. Looking around at everyone, he knew he would really miss the school and the happy times he'd had there.

'I take a lot of credit for Gareth's development,' Gwyn joked at the start of his presentation. 'If I hadn't banned him from using his left foot, he'd only be half the player he is now! But on a serious note, it's been an absolute pleasure to work with Gareth and I really do expect him to go on to bigger and better things. With his determination and good sportsmanship as well as his talent, he's an excellent role model to us all. Oh and he helped win us the Cardiff and Vale Senior Cup, of course!'

The whole Whitchurch football team were on their feet this time to cheer their success. Some even had their medals with them and waved them to the crowd. They were school celebrities now and boy, were they enjoying it. Winning the cup had been one of Gareth's happiest moments. To do it with his best friends, boys that he'd grown up with, was an amazing feeling that he'd never forget. It was also nice to give something back to the school that had been so supportive of his football talent. Up on the stage, Gwyn handed him the trophy and he lifted it high towards the ceiling.

Next, it was time for Gareth to make his speech. He'd been dreading this moment ever since he'd found out about winning the award. He hated public speaking and so he kept it as short as possible. 'Whitchurch High is a great school and a great sports school. Thank you to everyone here for all your support during my time here. I've really enjoyed it and it's a real honour to win this award.'

His friends wanted him to say something funny but he couldn't stop shaking, let alone tell a joke. Playing in an important football match was one thing, but making a speech in front of lots of people was something very different. He returned to his seat, red-faced but proud of what he'd achieved.

He was leaving with six GCSEs, including a Grade

A in PE. 'I would hope so,' his dad had said when he showed him the results. 'If you'd got a B in that, I would have kicked up a fuss!' Gareth knew no-one should rely on a career in football and therefore studying was essential. One more bad injury and he might have to look for a normal job, where his education would be very important.

As the pupils all walked out of the assembly hall and into the warm summer sun, Gareth felt sad about the changes that were about to happen in his life. To take up his football scholarship he was moving to Southampton, where he would be more than two hours away from his friends, family and of course Emma. He'd be able to come home quite often and everyone could come and visit him too, but it wouldn't be the same. As he and Emma often joked, they were 'homebirds' – moving away from Wales would be a very big deal.

'Don't worry about us,' Emma told him over dinner one night, when he was looking really sad. His days in Whitchurch were running out and they were spending as much time together as possible.

'You've got this incredible opportunity and you're going to be brilliant. I love you and I'm not going anywhere.'

Gareth smiled – his girlfriend had a great way of making him feel better about everything. 'Thanks, I love you too. We'll just have to watch *The X Factor* separately and then discuss it on the phone!'

Southampton would be a big new city to get used to but at least he'd be living with Theo, who was a local boy and would be able to show him around. He'd also spent enough time there at the academy to know it quite well.

Not that he was going there as a tourist, though – he had a job to do. He was there to follow in Theo's footsteps as the 'next big thing'. In April that year, 2005, he'd been a substitute in the FA Youth Cup Final, where his friend set up both of Southampton's goals. Together, Gareth and Theo would work hard and play hard as they chased their dreams. It certainly wouldn't be easy but they were both determined to be the best.

'Just you wait,' Theo told him after training one night. 'In a year, we'll be the stars of the Southampton team!'

CHAPTER 12

GROWING PAINS II

At first, the move to Southampton was difficult. Living with Theo was great fun but the football didn't go as well as he'd hoped. Gareth had proved in that game against Norwich that he was good enough to earn a scholarship but he was still in the middle of a major growth spurt. Every month he seemed to grow another inch taller. When he left Whitchurch High School, he was five foot eight inches – a few months later and he was getting close to six foot! His dad had been right but it wasn't all good news. The back pains were still troubling him, especially as he was playing more and more football at the academy.

'I'm fine when I'm jogging and when I'm
running at medium speed but when I try to sprint,
it really, really hurts,' he told the physio one day at
Staplewood during yet another session. 'My body just
won't let me do it.'

The physio had one word of advice for Gareth
– 'Patience'. Over the years, so many people had
told him this – his parents, Rod, his uncle Chris, his
coach at Cardiff Civil Service, Gwyn, Georges – but
it didn't make it any easier. In the yearly sprint tests,
he only came seventh.

'Once you stop growing, you'll be quicker than
ever,' Georges assured him afterwards. 'Plus, you
were miles ahead of everyone else on the Yo-Yo test.
Your stamina is brilliant!'

While Gareth struggled, Theo went from strength
to strength. All of the Southampton coaches were
talking about him and scouts from Manchester
United, Arsenal and Chelsea were watching him
play each week. There were rumours that even Real
Madrid were interested! Gareth was really pleased
for his friend but he couldn't help feeling a little bit

jealous of the attention he was getting. He watched from the stands as Theo became Southampton's youngest-ever player. He had only just turned sixteen. Luckily, however, his friend never lost sight of their plan.

'We're doing this together, Gareth! Soon, we'll both be playing for the first team, me on the right wing and you on the left. The Championship won't be able to handle us!'

This spurred Gareth on and things began to fall into place. He was now just over six feet tall and stronger than ever thanks to the exercises he was doing in the gym. The pains were almost gone too. The Southampton physio confirmed the good news. 'Eight inches in eighteen months, then no inches in the last two months – Gareth, I think you've finally stopped growing!'

Not only this, but his pace was getting better, too. Week after week, he got faster over short distances. He'd been the second fastest eleven-year-old in Wales – so speed was in his blood. As his confidence grew, his performances improved.

He was playing for both the Under-18s and the reserves, sometimes at left back and sometimes on the left wing. He still preferred to attack but he was also getting better in defence.

'I was chatting with some of the coaches at training this morning,' Theo told him one night as they sat playing FIFA. 'They were talking about a Welsh winger who was playing really well for the reserves.'

Gareth was so distracted that he let Theo score a goal. They paused the game. 'Really?'

Theo laughed at this – he was always telling his friend that he needed to believe in himself more. 'Yes, they were taking bets on when you'd get your debut!' he replied. 'Jim said May, Gary said August.'

Gareth's heart was beating so fast – he'd been dreaming of playing for Southampton ever since he made that first trip to the Bath academy when he was nine years old. According to Theo, that dream now looked like becoming a reality. He didn't tell anyone yet, however; Gareth didn't want to tempt fate. If he kept playing well, he knew his chance would come.

However, some sad news came first. Just when Gareth and Theo were making plans to get a flat together, his friend signed for Arsenal. It was an amazing opportunity for him to play for one of the biggest clubs in the world, but Gareth would really miss Theo. Still, if his friend could become a Premier League star, so could he. 'You'll be joining me in no time,' he told Gareth as they said their goodbyes.

In the end, Gareth's debut came sooner than anyone predicted. With Southampton safe in mid-table with only a few games left in the season, the manager decided it was time to test some youngsters. He'd been told that Theo wasn't the only promising player coming through the Southampton academy. Amongst the youth team, rumours were flying. Nathan Dyer had already made his debut but who else would be picked?

Gareth kept his fingers firmly crossed for weeks. Then after training one Thursday in April 2006, he got the brilliant news he'd been waiting for. The reserves coach was announcing his team for the weekend. As the names were read out, Gareth noticed he wasn't there – not at left back, not at left midfield and not on the bench. The coach saw the worry on his face and laughed. 'Sorry Gareth, you're not in the team this week.' He paused. 'Congratulations, you're playing for the first team against Millwall on Monday night instead!'

CHAPTER 13

THE DEBUT

Gareth couldn't wait to let everyone know the big news. Aged sixteen years and 273 days, he would become Southampton's second youngest ever player, after Theo.

'That's brilliant, son! We're so proud of you,' his parents cheered down the phone.

'Wow, this is so exciting!' Emma screamed. 'Well done, you've been working so hard for this. How does it feel?'

'Amazing!' he replied.

Emma travelled down to Southampton with Ellis and Gareth's parents and sister. There was no way any of them were going to miss his debut.

'Oh Gareth, you could have at least got a haircut for your big day!' his mother complained when they met for dinner the night before the game. 'You look so scruffy.'

Despite the nagging, it was great to have his family around to take his mind off things.

Gareth didn't sleep well that night. When he finally fell asleep, he dreamt that he scored an own goal in the last minute with the score at 0-0. He was very relieved to wake up and realise it was just a nightmare. He wiped away the sweat and got himself a glass of water. 'It's just another game,' he told himself.

He was shaking with nerves as he took his place in the dressing room the next day. One by one, the senior players came over to say hello. 'Welcome to the team, Gareth,' said the Saints captain, Claus Lundekvam, nearly crushing his hand. He felt like a boy amongst men. 'I've heard very good things about you! Don't be nervous today. I'll be right there alongside you to talk you through it.'

Gareth had been to the St Mary's Stadium lots

of times but it had never felt as big as it did as he warmed up on the pitch. 'Don't panic,' he muttered to himself, before carrying on with the passing drill. In the tunnel before kick-off, he closed his eyes and took a long, deep breath. He was ready for this, ready to start working from the Number 37 shirt they'd given him towards the all-important Number 3. Running out on to the pitch as a Southampton player was the new greatest experience of his life.

Oh when the Saints! the Northam Stand began and the rest of the home support joined in. *Oh when the Saints, Oh when the Saints go marching in, I want to be in that number, when the Saints go marching in!* Even though it was only half full, the stadium sounded so loud. With the fans behind him, Gareth felt like he could do anything.

With Millwall fighting to stay in the Championship, though, it was a tough game for a youngster. They played a very physical game, with lots of long balls up to their powerful attackers. As a skinny left back, Gareth had to be brave and focused. He felt more and more comfortable with each touch of the ball and even used his pace to get forward down the wing a few times. A penalty early on gave Southampton the lead and a late second sealed the win. Gareth was so pleased to get a victory and a clean sheet on his debut. He played the full ninety minutes and he would have happily played ninety more.

At the final whistle, Gareth did a full lap of the pitch, clapping the fans who had cheered him on and made his first game so special. He looked for his family in the crowd but there were far too many faces. Claus gave him a big bear hug as they went down the tunnel. 'You're a natural!'

The manager praised him in the changing room. 'Great game, lad. Very solid and composed – are you sure you're only sixteen?' he joked. Gareth was buzzing with joy.

Gareth didn't like the taste of alcohol, but he was certainly in the mood to celebrate. Once he'd showered and changed into his tracksuit, he found his personal fan club waiting for him. In their Southampton shirts with his name on the back, they looked just as happy as him.

'Well done, son. Great stuff!'

'You were so brilliant!'

'Nice performance mate – first of many!'

He was so glad to share his biggest day with his favourite people. Rod came over to say congratulations and there was a text message from Theo that read '2-0, eh? What a debut!' Gareth couldn't stop smiling – he was on cloud nine. After so many years of imagining it, it had finally come true. He was now officially a professional footballer.

At dinner, he sat there replaying the game in his head as the others talked around him. No, he couldn't remember making any big mistakes. He could do a lot better but it was a very good start. The ninety minutes had gone by so quickly. He couldn't wait to do it all again.

CHAPTER 14

THE STAR OF ST MARY'S

There was just enough time for Gareth to play one more game for the Southampton first team before the end of the season. Again it took place at home in front of the brilliant St Mary's crowd and again the Saints won 2-0. Two games, two wins, two clean sheets – Gareth was very pleased with his impact so far. He was still learning how to defend against bigger and more experienced players but he certainly wasn't letting the team down.

'You're a lucky charm!' Claus told him on the pitch afterwards as they thanked the crowd for their support. *Baaaale! Baaaale!* The fans were chanting his name. They had welcomed him in very quickly – he was one of the team now.

It had been an unbelievable end to the season for Gareth. In May, things got even better. One day as he was relaxing back in Whitchurch, he got a phone call.

'Hello, Gareth,' a very serious Welsh voice said. 'I hope you're well. I'm calling to say congratulations, you've been included in John Toshack's Wales squad for the upcoming friendly against Trinidad and Tobago.'

At first, Gareth thought it must be a joke – perhaps Ellis or Theo was playing a prank on him. He'd only played 180 minutes of league football; why would the national team be interested in him? However, it turned out to be real. Even when the man on the phone told him where to go to join up with the team, he still didn't really believe it. As it all sank in, he rushed off to spread the news. He was off to play for his home country of Wales in Graz, Austria.

'What a crazy six weeks it has been!' Gareth told

his dad, reflecting on his rise to league and then international football. He was finding it hard to sit still and Frank was just as excited and proud.

'You're hot property now, son. Wales want to make sure you don't go and play for England instead!' he joked over a cup of tea.

'No way!' was Gareth's instant response. It hadn't even crossed his mind. His mum's mum was English but he felt Welsh through and through. Playing for his country and wearing that big red dragon on his shirt was something he'd dreamt about for years. He'd grown up around Cardiff and his uncle Chris had played football for them. Ryan Giggs and John Hartson were his heroes, not Paul Scholes and Michael Owen.

Gareth travelled to Graz with a very young Welsh squad, because players like Giggs and Craig Bellamy were injured. The idea of training and playing with senior professionals like Rob Earnshaw and Simon Davies was still quite scary, so it was nice to see so many familiar faces from his time with the Under-18s and Under-21s. 'Welcome, good to have you with

us,' Lewin Nyatanga said, acting as if he'd been in
the team for years.

'Shut up you!' Gareth replied, giving him a friendly
punch on the arm. 'You're less than a year older than
me and you only have one cap!'

Lewin and Gareth were both on the bench for the
first half against Trinidad and Tobago. It was a pretty
boring start to the game, so Gareth decided to wind
his friend up a bit.

'Lewin, did you know that if I come on today I'll
beat your record?' Gareth nudged him and pretended
to count it out on his fingers. 'I'm nearly 250 days
younger than you were!'

'It's not age that matters, mate. It's talent,' Lewin
answered and then squirted him in the face with
water. It was good to have a laugh because Gareth
was so tense that his hands wouldn't stop shaking.
Everything was happening so fast for him.

It was 1-1 at half-time and the manager made
three substitutions. 'Start warming up, lad! You
should be on pretty soon,' one of the coaches
shouted as the game kicked off again. As Gareth ran

up and down the touchline, he tried to calm himself and stop his heart from beating so fast. This was a massive opportunity for him to impress and to repay the manager's faith in his ability. Wales were playing a 3-5-2 formation, which meant that he would play as a wing back with more freedom to move forward down the wing. He couldn't wait to get out on the pitch.

Ten minutes into the second half, Gareth was called, and became Wales's youngest ever international. He'd had so many unforgettable moments recently but this was definitely his proudest yet. As usual, the nerves disappeared as he took up his position on the left. He was so eager to do well but the team was struggling to attack. 'Gareth!' the manager shouted and pointed towards the opposition goal – the message was 'Get forward!'

With time running out, Earnshaw played a good ball out to Gareth and he found himself in space for the first time. It was the moment to bring the game to life. With a quick burst of pace, he ran past two defenders and pulled the ball back for Earnshaw

to shoot low past the goalkeeper. *Gooooaaaaalllll!*
Earnshaw went straight over to Gareth to thank him
for the pass, before performing his trademark front-
flip celebration.

With an assist on his international debut, now
Gareth really was the man of the moment. Or boy of
the moment – he was still only over a month away
from his seventeenth birthday. Danny Gabbidon, the
Wales captain, had even compared him to Wayne
Rooney. After the match, the media asked him for
an interview. How could he explain what he was
feeling? 'It feels like a dream come true!' was all he
could say.

Gareth didn't relax over the summer; instead, he
worked harder than ever. If he could stay fit and get
a bit stronger, he had a good chance of becoming
Southampton's first-choice left back. He was already
moving towards that Number 3 shirt, swapping '37'
for '22'.

'How's it going? How's the back feeling?' Rod
shouted one day to Gareth while the youth was
practising his free-kicks at the Staplewood Training

Ground. The team session had ended nearly an hour before and he was the last one out there. The goal he was shooting at was full of balls.

'It feels great at the moment! How's *your* back?' Gareth asked with a laugh as he sent yet another ball into the net.

'You're a rude little so-and-so – all the support I've given you over the years and that's how you thank me!' he said with a big smile. 'I was coming over to wish you luck for the season but maybe I won't bother.'

Rod was very happy to see Gareth doing so well. Even when he was in a lot of pain and Southampton were thinking of letting him go, he had never given up. For that determination alone, he deserved this success.

Gareth was in the starting line-up for the first game of the new season away at Derby. Gareth went on a few runs down the left but the team was struggling to create good chances. The manager wasn't happy. 'The holidays are over, lads!' he shouted at them. Fifteen minutes into the second half, Southampton

won a free-kick in a really good position near the
Derby goal. It was slightly to the right of the penalty
area, so perfect for a left-footed player.

Gareth had been practising free-kicks since he
was six years old, and so he was known for his great
scoring record in the youth teams. 'Give it a go!' his
teammate Rudi Skacel said as they stood over the
ball. The midfielder was a very good free-kick taker
too but Gareth didn't need to be told twice. Though
Rudi stood as if he was going to take it, Gareth then
took a few steps forward, and whipped the ball over
the wall and into the top corner.

As soon as the ball left his foot, Gareth knew it
was a goal. He'd hit it perfectly, with just the right
amount of power, curl and dip. After watching it
fly into the back of the net, he ran towards the fans
with his arms out wide like an aeroplane. What
a feeling. In the moment, he didn't quite know
how to celebrate – he raised a finger to his lips to
cheekily shush the Saints fans, then he jumped and
spun in mid-air. Finally, his teammates caught up
and piled on top of him.

The game finished 2-2. It hadn't been Gareth's greatest game but he'd scored his first Southampton goal. He was off the mark.

CHAPTER 15

THE NEW WELSH WIZARD

It didn't take long for Gareth to score his next goal – he did so in his very next game, in fact. With the Saints drawing 0-0 against Coventry City and the supporters growing restless, they won a free kick in front of goal. 'I've got this!' Gareth said immediately and no-one argued with him. It was a bit further out this time but he was full of confidence. He took three steps towards the ball and curled it straight into the top right corner again. There was no way the goalkeeper could save it.

Two great goals in two games! This time, Gareth ran to the fans by the corner flag with both arms raised above his head. Bradley Wright-Phillips jumped on his back and Rudi jumped on too. *Baaaale! Baaaale!* There was no feeling in the world like scoring a goal, especially in front of the home fans.

They went on to win 2-0 and the talk afterwards was all about Gareth. Southampton had some very talented youngsters: first Theo and now him. Would this new Welsh wizard become the next player to make a big money move to the Premier League? Not according to the manager. 'Gareth signed a contract and we want him to stay. The big clubs will not be getting him,' he told the media after the game.

'Dad, I'm happy here,' Gareth said at dinner that night. 'I'm still learning and this is a great place to learn.' It was crazy how quickly things changed in football – only eighteen months after that make-or-break Norwich match, and now apparently Manchester United wanted to buy him.

'I agree, son,' his dad replied, taking a sip of beer. 'You're too young to go and sit on the bench for a big club. You need to be playing football every week.'

Emma felt the same way. 'I don't feel you're ready

for that yet. Give it a year and if it's still going this well, then you can think again.'

Gareth nodded at this wise advice. Thank goodness he had people around him who would keep his feet on the ground. He needed to ignore the rumours and just play his normal game. That was easier said than done, however.

'Man, you could be winning the Premier League title in May!' teammate Nathan Dyer said as they warmed up against West Bromwich Albion. Gareth was playing against one of his childhood heroes, Welsh striker John Hartson. Weeks later, he would play with Ryan Giggs for the national team against Brazil. It was still hard to believe it was all real.

Even so, Gareth remained focused. 'No, I want to be winning the Championship title with Southampton in May,' he replied.

In October 2006, Gareth became the Wales national team's youngest-ever goal scorer. Facing Slovakia in the qualifiers for Euro 2008, Wales won a free kick in a great area. Gareth was only seventeen but there was no question that he would take it.

And there was no chance that the goalkeeper could save it. *Goooooooaaaaaaaallllllllllll!* It was his first international goal, although it was the only good moment in a 5-1 defeat. Gareth hated being on the losing side.

Every time he stepped up to take a free kick now, people expected him to score. 'The goalkeepers don't even move anymore – they know there's nothing they can do!' his teammates joked. Gareth was the talk of British football. Roy Keane called him 'an exceptional player'.

'You're a star now, mate!' Ellis told Gareth when they caught up after Christmas. 'The newspapers are saying that Ryan Giggs has told Sir Alex Ferguson to buy you in the January transfer window. Imagine that – Gareth Bale signs for Manchester United!' Ellis had always known that his best friend was a very talented player but even he was surprised by just how good he'd become in the past year.

'Ellis, surely you know by now that they usually talk rubbish!' Gareth responded. He was trying hard not to think about these things. Playing in the

Premier League was a lifetime dream for him but he wanted to do that with Southampton first, if possible. He owed them that. The Saints were in the playoff spots and playing well, with Gareth barely missing a game. He loved being a starter but this was his first season and his body was starting to get tired.

'Rest up and I'll tell the manager to give you a little break,' said the physio in the New Year. 'You're playing too much football for a seventeen-year-old.'

'No way – I can handle it!' Gareth replied, jumping to his feet. The last thing he wanted was a spell on the sidelines, watching his teammates winning games without him.

Gareth's defending was getting better and he was adding strength to his speed and skill.

'You're filling out a bit now, mate,' Claus joked in the gym one day. 'When you first came in, you were as skinny as a twig. Now, you're more like a small tree branch!'

The awards came thick and fast. In December 2006, he had won the BBC Wales Young Sports Personality of the Year, then the Football League

Young Player of the Year the following March. He was also named in the Championship Team of the Year. The only thing left to win was promotion.

'I can't wait for the play-offs – first we play Derby and then it's West Brom or Wolves in the final at Wembley!' Gareth was desperate to get Southampton back to where they belonged: the Premier League.

'Even if we get promoted, you won't be here next year. You'll be up at Old Trafford!' teammate Bradley said, throwing one of his socks at him.

'Hey, all I'm thinking about is winning the play-offs,' Gareth said, throwing it back at Bradley. He was getting tired of these rumours. 'I've got no idea what'll happen next season.'

The first leg against Derby was at home and the St Mary's crowd was even louder than normal. The Saints started well and scored a great goal after seven minutes. Gareth was feeling good. They were playing nice, passing football but they just couldn't score a second goal. Then disaster struck three times in twenty minutes. First, Derby equalised to make it 1-1 at half-time. Worse, early in the second half,

Gareth went in for a tackle and felt a pain in his leg. It really hurt and there was no way he could carry on playing. What cruel timing it was. He was substituted and just two minutes later, Derby won a penalty and scored it to win 2-1.

It was a miserable day for Gareth and it ended with him hobbling out of the stadium on crutches. His family tried to take his mind off it but nothing worked.

'The physio says there's no chance of me playing in the second leg. That's my season over!' he told them as they helped him into the car. Tears filled his eyes.

He watched from the stands as the Saints won the second leg 3-2 but then lost on penalties. It was heartbreaking, especially knowing that he couldn't do anything to help his team. When he went into the dressing room afterwards, the mood was very low.

'Boys, you were brilliant tonight,' he said to try to cheer them up. He really felt their pain. Most of the players had their heads in their hands, and he went round patting everyone on the back. 'We were so unlucky to lose that. Next year, we'll win the league so that we don't even need the play-offs!'

No-one said a word. It was another season in the Championship for Southampton but where would Gareth be? Despite all his love for Southampton, he really didn't know.

CHAPTER 16

SIGNING FOR SPURS

'Gareth, Tottenham have made a bid for you,' Southampton's manager George Burley told him just days after the Saints had missed out on promotion. He'd been called into George's office and he knew it must be about a transfer. 'They're desperate to sign you. We were hoping to keep you for a bit longer but it's a good offer and they're a great club.'

Wow, an offer from a Premier League team! He hadn't even played fifty first-team games and he had a big decision to make. Spurs had been following him for a few years and were ready to spend good money on him. He needed to discuss it with Emma and his family.

'That's great news, son!' his dad said when Gareth told him. 'They've got a good side – Dimitar Berbatov, Aaron Lennon, Ledley King. You should speak to the club and see what they have to say. There's no harm in that. If you don't like it, you can just say no.'

He took his dad's advice and agreed to meet the Tottenham manager, Martin Jol. 'Gareth, we finished fifth last season and the aim for this year is Champions League football,' Martin told him at the club's training ground. His sense of ambition was clear and impressive. 'We've got a really strong group of players but we want to make it better. You're young but we think you're ready. We're not looking for a player who'll be good in a few years – we want someone who's good enough to play today!'

It sounded so exciting and Gareth was persuaded. He called his dad straight away. 'I liked them. They really want me and not just to sit on the bench for the next few years. They want me to challenge for the left back and left wing spots.' He could see himself playing at White Hart Lane.

His mum came on the phone to offer her advice. 'I think you're making the right decision, Gareth. Martin phoned here yesterday. He seemed a very nice man. I told him it was your decision but he clearly really wants you at the club.'

Only a few days later, Gareth was a Premier League player for Tottenham Hotspur. The initial transfer fee was only £5 million but there was another £5 million to come if he did really well. It was an absolute bargain for one of the hottest prospects in the world. 'I'm just excited to be coming to a massive club like Spurs,' he told the media as he posed with the shirt. He had decided on Number 16, as it matched his birthday (16 July). Lee Young-pyo wore Number 3 for now but Gareth was determined to earn it from him as soon as he could.

On the day of the announcement, he got a text from Theo – by then at Arsenal – saying, 'Welcome to the best league in the world, mate. We're North London rivals now!' Theo had already told him that the atmosphere at the Arsenal-Spurs derby was the best thing he'd ever experienced, and now Gareth couldn't wait. He got goosebumps just thinking about it.

Even though he had only been at Southampton for just over a year, Gareth was very sad to say goodbye to the club. There had been so many ups and downs but the Saints had stuck by him through everything, and Gareth was so grateful for that support. He just wished that he'd got them into the Premier League before leaving, but at least his sale was giving them some much-needed money.

Rod, Southampton's talent scout who had discovered Gareth, was there at the training ground on his last day. He had a big smile on his face and rightly so. If it wasn't for him, Gareth would not have made it to the top. 'Well done, lad! I always knew you had it in you. You've got what it takes.' They hugged and Gareth thanked him for everything. As they parted, Rod winked and said, 'Oh and start learning Spanish now!' He knew all about Gareth's ultimate dream – to play for Real Madrid.

That would have to wait, however. For now, he was desperate to do well at Tottenham and

continue his development. He made his debut in
a friendly but picked up a thigh injury late in the
game. Gareth feared the worst as he limped off the
pitch but the physio reassured him. 'Don't worry,
it's just a dead leg. It'll hurt for a bit but it's nothing
too serious.'

Gareth was very relieved to hear that but it did
keep him out of the team for over a month. His
return was timed to perfection: Spurs were to
face Manchester United at Old Trafford. He was
determined to show Tottenham that they'd made the
right choice, and to show Sir Alex that he'd missed
out by failing to sign him.

In the tunnel before the Manchester United game,
Gareth closed his eyes and focused. He'd been
dreaming about this since the age of three – playing
football in one of the biggest stadiums in the world.
What an opportunity it was. He would be starting on
the left wing, where he had the freedom to do what
he did best: attack, attack, attack.

Gareth's proud parents were in the stands
to watch his Premier League debut. It was an

amazing experience and he played well, setting up good chances with his free-kicks and crosses. Unfortunately, his teammates couldn't score any of them and Manchester United ended up winning. In the dressing room afterwards, all of the players sat in silence for what felt like hours. Eventually, manager Martin tried to lift their spirits.

'Lads, you played very well,' he said. 'You deserved at least a point from that game, maybe even a win. There's no need to panic – we're heading in the right direction. Today, we missed too many chances. Next week, we must do better.'

It was great to get back out on the pitch and start life as a Spurs player, but Gareth really hated to lose. Little did he know how long it would be before he'd win another game.

CHAPTER 17

THE CURSE OF BALE I

The next game was a trip across London to Fulham and again Gareth was picked on the left side of midfield. He was keen on this more attacking role, where he could really use his pace to create goals. As he stretched and practised his short sprints before the game, he was optimistic. He could tell it was going to be a good day.

Again and again Gareth made dangerous runs. Spurs were 2-1 up and causing all kinds of trouble. He would surely score soon. Then after sixty minutes, when Robbie Keane flicked the ball out to the left, Gareth was already on the run. As fast as lightning, he sped past the Fulham defence, took the ball into the area and coolly slotted it past the goalkeeper. *Gooooaaaaalllll!* He ran towards the Tottenham fans, raising his hands to whip them up into a frenzy. He was on his way to becoming a Spurs hero.

At the final whistle, Gareth couldn't believe it. 3-3 – how had they thrown it away? 'Defend from the front,' he'd always been told at Southampton. He still had some work to do to get used to the Premier League.

'Well played, Gareth,' Martin said as they left the dressing room. 'You deserved to be on the winning team today.' It was nice to hear praise from his new manager but it was a win that he really wanted.

Next up was the match he'd been looking forward to most: the North London derby against Arsenal. Gareth and Theo teased each other all week in their text messages. 'We'll go top when we win!' Theo wrote the night before the game. It would be really upsetting for whoever lost.

Tottenham won a free-kick within shooting range. It was suitable for a right-footed player but Gareth wasn't going to let Younes Kaboul take it. He calmly swept his hair to the side and considered his options. He noticed that the Arsenal goalkeeper was standing towards the left of his goal and so he quickly swept the ball over the wall and low inside his right-hand post. *Gooooaaaaalllll!*

Gareth slid towards the corner flag on his knees, just as he had done as a young kid in the park. It didn't get better than this – he had scored the opening goal against their greatest rivals. 'Man, that was such a clever shot!' Robbie said. What a shame that Tottenham lost the game in the end. A month later, they dropped down into the relegation zone of the Premier League.

'It's not looking good,' Gareth told Ellis after an awful 3-1 defeat to Newcastle. Not only had they lost, but he had hurt his foot in an early tackle. He was on crutches again and they were hoping that there weren't any broken bones. At the final whistle, the fans booed the team and called for Martin the manager to be sacked. 'I can't really explain it – we've got good defenders but we keep making silly errors,' Gareth said. Martin was soon dismissed, and replaced as manager by Juande Ramos.

When Gareth returned from injury, Juande wanted him to play at left back. He would need to go back and work hard on his defending again.

'I love getting forward on the wing,' he told his dad on the phone one night, 'but I'll play wherever the manager tells me to. I just want to be out there on the pitch!'

A few weeks later, Gareth went in for a tackle and got kicked around the top of his right foot. He had never felt pain like it. Yet another injury, and he could tell straight away this one was serious. Afterwards, the whole team crossed their fingers for good news but Gareth had been right to fear the worst. 'It's not good, I'm afraid,' the physio reported to the dressing room. 'There's ligament damage to his ankle. He'll be out for at least three months.'

Gareth couldn't believe it – just when he was back in the team and playing well. The injury would require surgery to put a metal pin in his ankle. There would then be lots of boring rehab.

'This is going to be tough for you, I know,' Emma comforted him that night, 'but I'll be here for you. We can eat at Nando's and watch lots of films together! Then after a few weeks, you'll be back in the gym and working hard to get back to your best.' Gareth was grateful for his girlfriend's support but he was really upset.

He had plenty of time to think about his start at Tottenham. He felt that he'd played pretty well before the injuries but he still hadn't won a Premier League match. He was trying to ignore any talk of a jinx but what if it was true? Without him, Spurs made it to the League Cup Final after beating Arsenal 5-1. He was too sad to even text Theo about it.

The final took place in late February 2008 at Wembley. A tiny part of Gareth was hoping he might be fit in time to play but in the weeks before, he received bad news: the physio told him that his season was over. It was very hard to watch his teammates play so well and beat Chelsea in the final without him. Obviously, he was really happy for the boys but he didn't feel part of their success.

His teammates were all out on the pitch after lifting the trophy and it was time for their media pictures. 'Gareth, get in the photo!' Aaron Lennon shouted to him, holding up the medal around his neck with a huge grin on his face.

Gareth tried to say no but he had no choice: Tom Huddlestone came over and started spraying him with champagne. In his smart suit, Gareth stood towards the back on the left, doing his best to look happy. He told himself he'd be back at Wembley soon, and next time he would be on the pitch.

'Stay positive, work hard' – this was the simple message that Rod sent him as the season came to an end. Others had tried to cheer him up but this was just the kick he needed. It was time for him to look forward and set himself targets. If he couldn't run, he would build up his strength instead.

'Emma, I'm sorry for being such hard work recently,' he said over dinner. 'Let's go away on holiday and when we come back, I'll focus on next season.' Emma smiled – this was the Gareth she knew and loved.

CHAPTER 18

THE CURSE OF BALE II

'Mate, have you seen Jose Mourinho's fantasy football team?' Ellis asked on the phone a few days before the new season. 'You're in at left back!'

'Really?' Gareth couldn't believe it – what an honour to be picked by the Special One.

'Yes, he says, "Ashley Cole is the best left-back in English football but Bale shows the same instincts and has a brilliant left foot." How cool is that?!'

It was very cool indeed, and just the kind of encouragement Gareth needed. With his Number 3 shirt and a new contract, he was raring to go. It was time to end the jinx with a first Premier League win.

But the reality would be different. Two months later, Tottenham sat at the bottom of the Premier League after their worst ever start to a Premiership season. Not only had he still not participated in a winning game for the club, but in the match against Stoke City, he had been given the first red card of his career. He didn't think he was playing badly but the press kept talking about 'The Curse of Bale'. When he played, Spurs never won, but surely it wasn't all his fault?

After a year as Tottenham's manager, Juande Ramos would be replaced. 'I hear Harry Redknapp is going to be our new manager!' Aaron said with excitement. Gareth liked the sound of Harry; players loved playing for him and he knew the English game very well.

'I don't mind who it is, as long as he's good and he stays for a long time,' he replied. 'I hate all this change!'

Spurs won their first game under Harry, but Gareth was suspended from the team. 'I'm starting to think this curse is real,' Gareth told Emma after watching the game from the stands. 'There's no way he's going to want me in his team!'

Harry put an arm around Gareth at training one day. 'Kid, it's hard to leave you out but I'm trying to find the right balance in the team. I need Benoît Assou-Ekotto at left back and at the moment, Aaron and David are my first-choice wingers. We need strength if we're going to move up the table. Your chance will come, I promise.'

The young player knew he had to be tougher on the pitch. To improve his defending skills, he worked extra-hard with the Spurs coaches. He wanted to do everything he could so that he would take his next chance with both feet!

Gareth was desperate to come off the bench in the League Cup Final, especially after missing out the previous year. When he came on in extra-time, he tried to stay calm but in his head, he was already picturing himself scoring the winning goal. How amazing that would be. The match went to penalties and Gareth was ready to take one. In the end, however, he wasn't needed.

'Never mind, lad,' Harry said after Gareth had collected his runners-up medal. 'You'll be back here soon as a winner, I'm sure of it.'

Gareth tried to stay positive but it was difficult. Twenty-four league games without a win – it was an awful record. What if Spurs did want to get rid of him? He needed to break the jinx as soon as possible. Then disaster struck again in training. He felt a bad pain in his knee as he ran towards the ball. 'I'm sorry,' the physio told him. 'I know it's the last thing you want to hear, but you'll be out for at least a month.'

He'd need more surgery and miss the important build-up to the next season. Could things get any worse? Could he deal with more rehab? Would Spurs ever want him back?

His friends and family tried to raise his spirits.

'You'll be fine, Gareth – it's only a few weeks.'

'At least the season's over and you'll be back before the next one!'

'Remember, you've only just turned twenty – you've got years ahead of you!'

Nothing really helped, though. What Gareth really needed was some luck. Thankfully, better times were just around the corner.

CHAPTER 19

BREAKING THE JINX

'Gareth, get ready. You're coming on!' Harry
shouted, with Tottenham 4-0 up. It was a great
chance for Gareth to get that first win, even if he
was only a substitute. He was desperate to play again
before the team forgot all about him.

'Even you can't curse this one!' Aaron Lennon
joked as Gareth replaced him in the squad. In fact,
Spurs scored one more with him on the pitch.
Afterwards, Gareth celebrated like he'd scored a hat-
trick – it felt so great to be on a winning team.

'That's the first of many, mate!' David Bentley
told him.

He still needed that first full Premier League

victory, however. When Benoît Assou-Ekotto suffered an injury, it meant Gareth was back in the team at last – and when Tottenham beat Fulham 2-0 in January 2010, a massive weight was lifted off his back. Gareth had not scored at Tottenham since September 2007, but he was no longer the club's curse.

'It's over!' Emma shouted for joy at the final whistle.

'We'll need to find someone else to blame when we lose now!' Harry told Gareth in the dressing room after the game.

There was no stopping him now. He had the confidence to match his talent and there was no way Harry could drop him, even when Benoît was fit again. So, what could he do?

'Gareth, I still think your best position is left back but we need Benoît out there too,' Harry told him after training ahead of their match against Blackburn. 'So we're going to try you on the left wing.'

Gareth was over the moon at the news. He loved playing on the wing, where he could really use his pace and skill to attack. 'This is it, Ellis,' he told his best friend. 'I can feel it – big things are about to happen.'

In the match, Gareth was unstoppable. Again and again, he flew past the right-back to set up chances for the strikers. Every time he got the ball, he looked dangerous. Spurs won 3-1, and Gareth was the one everyone was talking about afterwards. It was nice to be getting attention for the right reasons again.

Suddenly, every time Gareth played, Tottenham won. All he needed now was goals. Playing on the wing, he was getting more chances but he couldn't find the net. 'Kid, you're on fire at the moment. Don't worry about goals – give it time and you'll be scoring left, right and centre,' Harry told him. It was really nice to have a manager who really believed in him.

When Gareth's long-awaited goal finally came, it was April 2010, in the biggest game of the season against Arsenal. Tottenham were fifth in the table and their rivals were third – so it was a tense battle for Champions League places at White Hart Lane.

Spurs were 1-0 up after ten minutes, and then one minute into the second half, Gareth made a great striker's run towards the penalty spot. The Arsenal defenders weren't marking him. He put his hand in the air, calling for the ball, and Jermain Defoe found him with the perfect pass. From about six yards out, Gareth coolly slotted past the keeper with his left foot. *Gooooaaaaalllll!*

The crowd went wild and Gareth ran towards them, his arms above his head. What a match to score in! Arsenal pulled one goal back with five minutes to go but Tottenham held on for the victory. Gareth's goal was the winner – it couldn't get better than that. Or could it? Three days later, against Chelsea, Gareth got the ball on the left side of the penalty area. He cut inside past the defender and smashed a low shot into the bottom corner... with his right foot! Again, his goal turned out to be the winner.

'I thought that leg was just for standing on!' Aaron joked after the game. Little did he know the story about Gwyn banning Gareth from using his left foot during school practices at Whitchurch High.

Gareth was so pleased to see the benefits of all that hard work. After two massive wins, there was a good chance he would be playing for Spurs in the Champions League next year.

With two games left that season, they still needed points against rivals Manchester City to finish fourth and so qualify for the UEFA Champions League in Europe. 'We've got to finish this season on a high,' Gareth told his teammates before the game. 'We deserve that fourth spot, so let's beat them!' In less than six months, he had gone from being the unlucky sub to one of the team's key figures. He played his heart out against City and with just minutes to go, Crouchy (aka Peter Crouch) scored the goal they needed. Spurs had done it – and it felt amazing to qualify for Europe.

After the game, Gareth celebrated with Emma and his parents. 'Well done, son, I always knew you'd turn things around!' his dad said, raising a glass to toast Gareth's success.

'I'm so proud of you,' said his mum, giving him a big hug. 'You never gave up and look at you now!'

This was only the start; Gareth was already looking towards the next goal. 'Just wait until they see me in September after a good pre-season,' he told Emma with a big smile on his face. 'I'm ready to become the best player in the Premier League.'

CHAPTER 20

NEW PLAYER, NEW CELEBRATION

In the first game of the 2010–11 season, against Stoke City, Gareth's first goal came off his nose, but his second was brilliant. As Aaron dribbled down the right wing, Gareth found himself alone on the far side of the penalty area. When the cross came in, Gareth struck it straight away on the volley. He hit it perfectly and the ball flew into the top corner – what a finish. *Goooooaaaaaaaalllllll!*

It was the best goal Gareth had scored yet. As he ran towards the fans, he had found a new way to celebrate. With his thumbs and index fingers, he formed the shape of a heart and lifted it up to show the crowd. It was for his teammates, his coaches, his fans, his family but above all, it was for the most important person in his life – Emma. Thanks to her love and support, he had never given up on his dream.

Gareth was a big deal now. In pre-season, everyone had noticed the difference in him. 'Gareth, I think that's enough,' the Spurs coaches had told him every day on the training field where he never stopped running. 'We don't want you to get another injury!'

'When we left for the summer, you were still a skinny kid,' David panted as he watched Gareth fly straight past him. 'Now, you're a proper man – it's scary how good you are!'

Gareth had added lots of muscle, which made him even faster. There was even more determination in his eyes and he was starting to look like a superstar. He had a new, stylish haircut and now he wore fashionable clothes rather than tracksuits.

'Who do you think you are?' Crouchy joked. 'David Beckham?'

Watching Andrés Iniesta, Lionel Messi and

Cristiano Ronaldo at the World Cup in South Africa
had given Gareth even more desire to become
a superstar. Making a name for himself in the
Champions League was the next massive step.

CHAPTER 21

TAXI FOR MAICON

It was October 2010 and Gareth faced his biggest
test yet. Tottenham were playing the European
champions, Inter Milan, in front of 80,000 fans at
the San Siro Stadium, and he was up against one
of the best defenders in European football, the
Brazilian-born Maicon. Not only this, but the Italian
giants had decided to play another brilliant right-
back, Javier Zanetti, in front of him to protect against
Gareth's speed.

'I've always wanted to play in games like this,'
he told Ellis when his friend asked if he was feeling
nervous. There was never any fear for Gareth these
days; instead, he was just excited to play against

the best in the world. These Champions League nights were so special – the music, the crowds, the cameras. Gareth was still only twenty-one years old and he was learning more with every game.

'Right now, you're very, very good,' Harry told his team before the match to inspire them, 'but if you win here tonight, you'll go down in Spurs history as great.'

Sadly, though, nothing went according to plan. After thirty-five minutes, Spurs were down to ten men and losing 4-0. At half-time, there was silence in the dressing room; everyone was in shock. 'OK boys, keep your heads up,' Harry said eventually. 'The plan for the second half is to not let them score any more. Then, if we get a few chances, maybe we can score one ourselves.'

Most people thought the game was done and dusted, but not Gareth. He had nothing to lose and people were watching him on television all over the world. 'Inter think this is over,' he said to himself. 'They won't be ready for me.'

All he needed was the ball. When Crouchy gave

it to him on the left, it was time to attack. Gareth
was still in his own half but he set off at top speed,
going past one defender, then another, like they
were statues. When he ran like that, no-one could
catch up with him, not even his own teammates.
As he reached the penalty area, a third defender
came across to try to make a tackle and Gareth
decided it was time to shoot. He fired the ball
powerfully like an arrow into the bottom corner.
Goooooaaaaaaaallllll!

It was an incredible strike but there was no time
to celebrate. There was still work to be done. Gareth
grabbed the ball from the net and ran back to the
halfway line. With just a couple of minutes to go,
Gareth was on the run again. The Inter defence
could only stand and watch as he sprinted into the
penalty area with the ball. He went for goal and
again he found the net. The Spurs fans were going
wild, but Gareth got up off the grass and calmly ran
back for the restart.

In stoppage time, he got the ball on the edge of
the box and found that bottom corner for a third

time. A hat-trick! Tottenham had been 4-0 down and now thanks to Gareth's goals it was 4-3! There was no time left to score the equaliser but in the space of ninety minutes, promising Premier League player Gareth had become an international superstar.

Gareth had always known that he could be brilliant at the highest level but even he was surprised by just how well the Inter Milan game had gone. He'd scored three goals in only his third Champions League game. Suddenly, everyone was talking about how much he was worth and which clubs wanted to buy him – Inter Milan, Juventus, even Real Madrid! Harry, however, wasn't selling his star. 'You couldn't buy him for £25 million or £30 million.'

Expectations were high by now. If he had one quiet game, people said Gareth wasn't that good. Now that he was Tottenham's biggest threat, Gareth needed to get used to the extra attention. 'Teams are trying all kinds of things to stop me, so I've got to think of other ways to get past them,' he explained to the Spurs coaches. To be the

best, Gareth knew he needed to play brilliantly in
every game.

Before the return match against Inter Milan at
White Hart Lane, Harry gave Gareth a few days off.
His star man had played a lot of football in the last
few months. He needed him and he needed him
fighting fit. 'Take a break, lad. Go to the beach and
get some sun!'

Instead, Gareth took Emma back to rainy Cardiff
to relax. 'This is what I call a holiday!' he joked with
his old friends over a meal at Nando's. He would
always be a homebird at heart.

'Apparently, Maicon was ill in the last game,'
Aaron told Gareth when he got back. 'On Tuesday
night, you'll need to remind him that the only bug
he's suffering from is you!'

The Inter defenders were told to stick to Gareth
like glue, but when Tuesday night came they
panicked every time he got the ball. Again and again,
he left them for dead with his speed and trickery.
The Italian giants just didn't know how to cope with
him. '*Taxi for Maicon!*' the Spurs fans sang at the

top of their voices. Gareth set up his team's second and third goals with his brilliant attacking runs and perfect crosses.

Spurs would win 3-1 against the European champions – and Gareth was so pleased to be on the winning team this time. Could anything beat this feeling? The TV pundits said it was one of the best performances they'd ever seen, and Real Madrid legend Luis Figo described Gareth as 'amazing'.

'Gareth, you might not have scored tonight,' Harry told him afterwards, putting an arm around him, 'but you were even better than in Milan!'

CHAPTER 22

THE NEXT BIG THING

'Wasn't ten goals your target for this season?' Ellis asked him when they met up at Christmas. While everyone else stuffed their faces with turkey, Gareth was careful not to eat too much. 'Well, you've done that and there are still five months to go. Plus, you've swung in 136 crosses – more than anyone else in the Premier League!'

Gareth celebrated the end of 2010 – his best ever year – with a goal on New Year's Day. It was an extra-special one – a header. Rafael van der Vaart hit a great free-kick towards goal and Gareth stood in the wall and flicked the ball past the goalkeeper. 'That was really clever,' Aaron told him after the game. 'You jumped like Cristiano Ronaldo!'

The newspapers were saying that Jose Mourinho wanted to sign Gareth for Real Madrid in the summer. Could it be true? Even if it was, there was no way the young man would let the fame and rumours go to his head. Gareth had grown up a lot in the last few years but he was still the shy lad from a quiet Welsh town who hated speaking in front of the cameras. 'I let my football do the talking,' he told journalists again and again. Gareth's focus was on staying fit and getting better and better.

It was difficult being the 'next big thing'. In every game, Gareth had two or three defenders marking him and there were plenty of rough tackles. He knew he had to be strong and wait for the perfect moment to work his magic. And with the opposition giving him special treatment, there was more space for Crouchy, Rafael and Luka Modrić.

'The worst thing you can do is get frustrated,' his dad reminded him after another tough away-draw.

'Just ignore all of the talk, get your head down and work harder than ever.'

In the Champions League quarter-finals in April 2011, Gareth got his dream fixture – a game against Real Madrid. On the day of the first match, he was awake at dawn like a child on Christmas Day. It was so exciting to be playing against such a legendary club, especially with Mourinho watching him.

However, just as against Inter in Milan, it all went wrong. Crouchy was sent off in the first few minutes and the *Galácticos* won 4-0. This time, there would be no repeat performance of Gareth's incredible second-half hat-trick.

'There's a second leg, remember!' Emma told him after the game, hoping to cheer him up a bit. 'You've got another chance next week to impress them.'

Unfortunately, despite his best efforts, Gareth couldn't save Tottenham from defeat. There was some positive news, though, as he was included on the shortlist for the PFA Player of the Year Award.

He turned up at the posh awards ceremony just hoping for a good night. 'There's no way I'll get more votes than great players like Carlos Tevez and Samir Nasri,' he said to Emma as they arrived on the red carpet. So when his name was read out as the winner, Gareth couldn't believe it. He was still in shock as he went up on to the stage to collect the trophy. 'This is a massive award and a great honour. Thank you,' he told the big dining room full of football legends.

It was a lovely reminder of just how far he'd come. In nine incredible months, Gareth had gone from reject to household name. Despite being the talk of Europe, Gareth never stopped improving himself, especially with the likes of Real Madrid showing an interest. He wanted more of everything: assists, headers and, most importantly, goals.

CHAPTER 23

THE BALE EFFECT

Before the 2012–13 season, Gareth made a bold decision that showed just how confident he felt in his ability. He was the club's star player now.

'I'm not a left back any more,' he told Spurs' new manager André Villas-Boas. 'I used to love the '3' shirt but now I need an attacker's number. Giggsy wore '11' so I'll take that now that Rafael's gone.'

There had been lots more rumours about a transfer to Real Madrid but Gareth was happy to be staying at White Hart Lane. He wanted another go at getting that Champions League spot. He owed Tottenham that for sticking by him through all of the injuries and the awful jinx.

BALE

It felt great to wear the number of a true left winger but André had different plans for Gareth. He wanted him to play all across the attack, sometimes on the wing and sometimes through the middle. Gareth loved his new free role. In a game against Manchester United, he dribbled all the way from the halfway line, leaving defenders trailing behind him, before finding the bottom corner. It was another one of those lightning-quick runs that Gareth was now famous for.

'That's the kind of goal I need to score more of,' he told his dad afterwards, still buzzing from the experience of winning at Old Trafford. 'Big goals in big moments of big games!'

The newspapers were calling it 'The Bale Effect'. If he wasn't saving the day for his club, he was saving the day for his country. In the 2014 World Cup qualifiers, Wales were playing Scotland at home at the Millennium Stadium. Nearly 70,000 fans sang the national anthem loud and proud, waving their red dragon flags, but Wales were 1-0 down with ten minutes to go. They really needed to win.

Gareth got the ball near the halfway line and off

he went, dribbling through four Scotland players at top speed. As he got into the box, a defender tripped him. Penalty! There was only one person who would take it. As the goalkeeper dived one way, Gareth coolly placed the ball in the other corner. To celebrate, he placed his trademark heart over the red dragon on his shirt. He loved scoring for his country.

There was still enough time for Gareth to score again. He ran with the ball towards the Scotland goal. At first, he moved at half-speed but then suddenly he sprinted past the tired defenders. He was a long way out but his shooting had never been better. He hit the ball perfectly and it flew like a rocket into the top corner. *Goooooaaaaaaaalllllll!* It was a world-class strike, the best he'd ever scored. He did 'The Klinsmann', diving onto the grass just like he used to do in his back garden as a kid. What a feeling, what a comeback.

'That was a one-man show out there!' joked his Welsh teammate Aaron Ramsey.

'No it wasn't!' insisted Gareth. 'We've got a good team now and we're starting to work well together.'

Playing in a big tournament with Wales was right at the top of Gareth's wish list. Another ambition was to score a hat-trick in a Premier League game. 'I've scored two goals loads of times but I've never got that third,' he told best friend Ellis, as they watched football on TV in Gareth's Essex home.

'You're right, it's a big deal,' Ellis agreed. 'Alan Shearer, Michael Owen, Thierry Henry, Cristiano Ronaldo – they've all got at least one!'

A potential opportunity would arise on Boxing Day 2011. Away at Aston Villa, with over half an hour to go, Spurs were 1-0 up, and Gareth knew they needed at least one more to secure the win. Suddenly, the ball came to him near the halfway line. He flicked it beyond the defender and sprinted to get to it first. There could only be one winner in that race! There was nothing the Villa defence could do, as Gareth dribbled around the goalkeeper and put the ball in the net.

'Right, let's get another!' he shouted to Aaron Lennon as they celebrated the goal. Ten minutes later, Gareth scored again. 'Right, let's get another!'

he shouted to Aaron again. 'Today's the day to get a third.'

Ten minutes later, Jermain found Gareth in a space just inside the penalty area. Gareth had to stretch for the ball, but he was successful, and sent it flying into the top of the net. Hat-trick! Finally, he could take the matchball home with him. Gareth had gone from left-back to left-wing; did this now make him a striker?

'I love scoring goals so much!' Gareth said to Emma that night as they looked after their two-month-old daughter, Alba. He really loved the new experience of fatherhood and the late nights and early mornings didn't seem to be affecting his form on the pitch. If anything, they seemed to be making him better. Gareth put the matchball on top of the Christmas tree and took a photo to send to his Twitter fans.

'If you had to choose between the goals and Alba and I,' asked Emma, 'what would you choose?'

He paused for a moment and then laughed. 'You two, of course!'

In May 2013, Gareth grabbed his twentieth league goal of the season. Slightly unfortunately, it was the winner against his old club, Southampton.

Rod, who had originally spotted Gareth's potential for the Southampton team, met up with him after the game. 'Wow, things have gone pretty well for you in the last few years!' he said. 'What's the plan?'

'What do you mean?'

'You could play for any club in the world now, Gareth. Manchester United? Bayern Munich? Barcelona? Real Madrid?'

'You know Real Madrid is the dream – let's see what happens this summer.'

'Well I hope you've been taking Spanish classes!'

CHAPTER 24

MOVING TO MADRID

'How much longer can this go on? What more is there to say?' Gareth asked his dad. The talks between Tottenham and Real Madrid seemed to be going on forever.

'Be patient, son. Spurs are just trying to get as much money as possible for their star man. It's only fair.'

It was 2013. Gareth had experienced six very eventful and sometimes happy years at Tottenham and they had helped him through some very difficult times. His year at Southampton had been vitally important in his development but at Tottenham he had become one of the best players in the world. He would never forget the memories of those amazing games against Inter Milan and Arsenal.

And all those goals... twenty-six in the last season alone. He had so many favourites – the last-minute winner against West Ham, the lightning-quick strike against Swansea City. Gareth had tried so hard to repay Tottenham by getting them back into the Champions League but again he couldn't quite do it. He just hoped the fans knew how much he loved them.

Gareth had won the PFA Player of the Year award twice in three years but what he wanted now was big club trophies. It was time to move on to the next chapter of his career, and he was so excited to become the next *Galáctico*. He would play on one wing, with Cristiano Ronaldo on the other, and Karim Benzema would be the striker. He was ready for that challenge.

'I want to win everything and at Real Madrid, I know I can do that,' he told Ellis. 'They have an amazing team and Luka's already there, so he will help me to settle in.' Manchester United were also

MATT AND TOM OLDFIELD

trying to sign him but Gareth had made up his mind. He had always loved the style and skill of Spanish football.

Finally, the deal was done. Gareth's childhood dream had come true. All of those hours practising in the park and the playground had been worth it. He would be wearing the most famous white shirt of all.

'I'm going to miss you guys a lot,' he told his Spurs teammates as he went to say his goodbyes. 'Thanks for everything and hopefully I'll see you in the Champions League very soon!'

'We didn't want to let you go,' the manager André Villas-Boas told him, 'but in the end we had no choice. We wish you all the best.'

In the end, Real Madrid had paid nearly £85 million for him, which was 100 million euros. Gareth was now the most expensive player in the world.

'That's crazy money! I can't believe it – it's more than they spent on Cristiano Ronaldo!' he said to Emma as they prepared to leave their house in Essex. 'I'll really have to prove myself in every game.'

He would need to score lots of goals and set up lots more with his dribbling and crossing. Despite his impressive twenty-six goals in his final season at Tottenham, he would need to score just as many next season, if not more. This was his biggest test yet but he felt ready.

His dad had no doubts either. 'You'll be great. Four years ago, Spurs nearly sold you to Newcastle and now you've signed for the biggest club in the world!'

It was time to go to Spain. Tomorrow, Real Madrid would present their record signing to thousands of fans at the Bernabéu Stadium. Gareth couldn't wait.

CHAPTER 25

WELCOME TO SPANISH FOOTBALL!

'We think you're ready to play on Saturday,' Gareth's new manager, Carlo Ancelotti, told him at training.

It was the good news he had been waiting for. Gareth had been at Real Madrid for nearly two weeks and he was desperate to make his debut.

'The weather here is great, my teammates are really nice and my Spanish is improving,' Gareth told Ellis on the phone, 'but I just want to play football now!'

'They've won three games out of three so far without you,' his best friend replied. 'I think you need to get back out on that pitch as soon as possible!'

Now recovering from a foot injury, Gareth had come off the bench for the Wales national squad earlier that week. The Madrid fans wanted to watch their record signing in action. It was time to start showing them why he was the most expensive player in the world.

Lining up as a Real Madrid player for the first time was an amazing feeling. Wearing the classic white shirt, with its history of trophies and world-class players, was a dream come true for Gareth. They didn't have as many fans away at Villarreal as they did back home at the Bernabéu Stadium but they still made plenty of noise as Gareth did his final stretches before kick-off. Emma and Alba were up there in the crowd and so were his parents. It was the biggest day of Gareth's career so far.

Right from the first whistle, the game was played at a very high speed, and after a period of injury, Gareth found it hard to keep up. 'To start with, keep it really simple,' he told himself. The first few times he got the ball, he passed it straight away. With opponents all around him, there was no chance to go on one of his brilliant dribbles. 'Welcome to Spanish football!' one defender joked as he helped Gareth back up to his feet after another tough tackle.

Gareth needed to get more involved and create some magic. 'Let's swap wings!' Cristiano shouted to him after half an hour, with Real Madrid 1-0 down. Gareth was very pleased to move back to the left, where he was at his most comfortable and most dangerous.

A few minutes later, Luka Modrić got the ball on the right of midfield and played it to Dani Carvajal just inside the penalty area. As Dani passed it across goal, Gareth made a great run at the back post and lost his marker. The timing was perfect and he slid the ball into the net. *Goooooaaaaaaaalllllll!* One by one, his new teammates ran over to celebrate with him. Gareth smiled his biggest smile and made the famous heart with his fingers and thumbs. It wasn't one of his best goals, but even so, he had scored on his debut for the biggest club in the world.

The boy had become a *Galáctico*.

Turn the page for a sneak preview of
another brilliant football story by
Matt and Tom Oldfield. . .

CRISTIANO RONALDO

Available now!

CHAPTER 1

EUROPEAN GLORY

Cristiano had already won so many trophies during his amazing career – one Spanish league title, two Spanish cups, three Premier League titles, three English cups, three Champions League trophies and three Ballon d'Ors. But he still felt something was missing. That something was an international trophy with Portugal.

And on 10 July 2016, he was one step away from achieving that dream. With his confidence and goals, Cristiano had led his team all the way to the Euro 2016 final. At the Stade de France, Portugal faced a France team with home advantage and world-class players like Paul Pogba and Antoine Griezmann.

Portugal were the underdogs, but they had the best player in Europe – Cristiano. And he had never been more determined to win.

After their coach, Fernando Santos, had given his team talk in the dressing room, it was time for the senior players to speak. Nani went first and then it was Cristiano's turn.

'We've done so well to get this far,' their captain told them. 'One more win and we will go down in history. We will return home as heroes!'

The whole squad cheered. Together they could become the champions of Europe.

Cristiano stood with his eyes closed for the Portuguese national anthem. He didn't mumble the words; he shouted them at the top of his voice. He loved his country and he wanted to do them proud on the pitch.

After seven minutes, Cristiano got the ball just inside the French half. As he turned to attack, Dimitri Payet fouled him. The game carried on but Cristiano was still on the ground, holding his left knee and screaming in agony.

Oww!

As the physios used the magic spray and rubbed his knee with an ice pack, Cristiano winced. The injury didn't look good. He put his hands to his face to hide the tears.

Dimitri came over to say sorry for his tackle, but Cristiano was too upset to reply. Eventually, he stood up and limped off the field. On the touchline, he tested his leg – it didn't feel good but he wanted to keep playing.

'Are you sure?' João Mário said to him as he walked back onto the pitch.

'I have to try!' Cristiano told him.

But a minute later, he collapsed to the ground. On his big day, Cristiano was in too much pain to continue. He kept shaking his head – he couldn't believe his bad luck.

'You have to go off,' Nani told him, giving his friend a hug. 'We'll do our skipper proud, I promise!'

Cristiano wasn't ready to give up yet, though. The physios put a bandage around his knee and he went back on again. But when he tried to run, he had to stop. He signalled to the bench: 'I need to come off'.

He ripped off his captain's armband. 'Wear this,' Cristiano said to Nani, putting the armband on him. 'And win this final!'

'Yes, we'll win this for you!' Pepe shouted.

As he was carried off on a stretcher, Cristiano cried and cried. The most important match of his life was over.

It was 0–0 at half-time and Cristiano was there in the dressing room to support his teammates. 'Stick together and keep fighting hard!' he told them.

In the second-half, he was there on the bench, biting his fingernails and, in his head, kicking every ball. Every time Portugal nearly scored, he was up on his feet ready to celebrate. Just before striker Éder went on as a sub, Cristiano looked him in the eyes and said, 'Be strong. You're going to score the winner.'

But after ninety minutes, it was still 0–0. Cristiano walked around giving encouragement to the tired players. It was tough not being out on the pitch, but he could still play his part. After 109 minutes, Éder got the ball, shrugged off the French defender and sent a rocket of a shot into the bottom corner.

Goooooooooooooaaaaaaaaalllllllllllllllllllll!!!!!!!!!!!

Cristiano went wild, throwing his arms in the air and jumping up and down. The whole Portugal squad celebrated together. They were so close to victory now.

For the last ten minutes, Cristiano stood with Santos as a second manager. He hobbled along the touchline, shouting instructions to the players.

Run! Defend! Take your time!

At the final whistle, Cristiano let out a howl of happiness as the tears rolled down his cheeks again. He hugged each of his teammates and thanked them.

'No, thank *you!*' Éder said to him. 'Without you, I wouldn't have scored that goal!'

'I told you we'd do it!' Pepe laughed.

Cristiano took his shirt off and threw it into the crowd. They had to give him another one so that he could do his captain's duty – collecting the Euro 2016 trophy.

He climbed the steps slowly, giving high-fives to the fans he passed. The trophy had red and green ribbons, the colours of Portugal's flag. As Cristiano lifted the trophy, the whole team cheered. He kissed it and then passed it on to the other players. No words could describe the joy that Cristiano was feeling.

It was at Manchester United and Real Madrid that he became a superstar, but Cristiano's incredible journey to the top of world football had begun at home in Portugal, with his family, on the island of Madeira. And so the Euro 2016 triumph was a way of saying thanks, for when life wasn't always easy growing up.

Without a difficult start in life, perhaps Cristiano wouldn't have had his amazing hunger to be the best, which turned a special gift into years of glory.

Real Madrid

🏆 UEFA Champions League: 2013–14

🏆 Copa del Rey: 2013–14

🏆 FIFA Club World Cup: 2014

🏆 UEFA Super Cup: 2014

Individual

🏆 FAW Young Player of the Year: 2007

🏆 Tottenham Hotspur Young Player of the Year: 2009–10, 2010–11

🏆 Wales Player of the Year Award: 2010, 2011, 2013, 2014

🏆 BBC Wales Sports Personality of the Year: 2010

🏆 BBC Wales Carwyn James Junior Sportsman of the Year: 2006

🏆 Premier League PFA Team of the Year: 2010–11, 2011–12, 2012–13

🏆 PFA Players' Player of the Year: 2010–11, 2012–13

🏆 PFA Young Player of the Year: 2012–13

🏆 FWA Footballer of the Year: 2012–13

🏆 UEFA Team of the Year: 2011, 2013

🏆 Premier League Player of the Month: April 2010, January 2012, February 2013

BALE

(11) THE FACTS

NAME:
Gareth Frank Bale

DATE OF BIRTH:
16 July 1989

AGE: 27

PLACE OF BIRTH:
Cardiff

NATIONALITY: Wales

BEST FRIEND: Ellis

CURRENT CLUB: Real Madrid

POSITION: RW

THE STATS

Height (cm):	**183**
Club appearances:	**397**
Club goals:	**127**
Club trophies:	**6**
International appearances:	**66**
International goals:	**26**
International trophies:	**0**
Ballon d'Ors:	**0**

★ ★ ★ **HERO RATING: 89** ★ ★ ★

GREATEST MOMENTS

Type and search the web links to see the magic for yourself!

6 AUGUST 2006,
DERBY 2-2 SOUTHAMPTON

https://www.youtube.com/watch?v=DWVRw4VmN9Q
On the opening day of the new Championship season, Gareth scored his first goal for Southampton. It was a brilliant, curling free-kick and the Derby goalkeeper had no chance. Gareth was only seventeen but he was already a real star for the future.

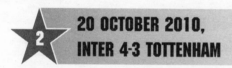

20 OCTOBER 2010, INTER 4-3 TOTTENHAM

https://www.youtube.com/watch?v=P82zf6hwORO

The night when Gareth became a superstar. After years of injuries and disappointments, his hard work paid off as he scored an incredible Champions League hat-trick. Gareth destroyed Inter's right-back Maicon with his pace and skill. Two weeks later, he did it again back at White Hart Lane.

20 NOVEMBER 2010, ARSENAL 2-3 TOTTENHAM

https://www.youtube.com/watch?v=ezxuD7MYDJQ&t=193s

Gareth scored lots of goals in the North London derbies against Arsenal but this was his most important. Tottenham were 2-0 down at the Emirates when Gareth started the comeback with a cool finish after a brilliant attacking run. Spurs went on to claim their first away victory over Arsenal in seventeen years.

 4   12 OCTOBER 2012, WALES 2-1 SCOTLAND

https://www.youtube.com/watch?v=QjxiN1OapRM

Gareth really loves playing for his country. In this World Cup 2014 qualifier, Wales were losing 1-0 but he never gave up. First, he won and then scored a penalty to make it 1-1. Then, in the 88th minute, Gareth dribbled forward and hit a phenomenal shot into the top corner to win the game for Wales.

5   14 SEPTEMBER 2013, VILLARREAL 2-2 REAL MADRID

https://www.youtube.com/watch?v=KXXhNmPbGHU

This wasn't Gareth's best goal but it was a very special moment to score on his Real Madrid debut. After his £85 million transfer, he needed to show that he was good enough to be a Galáctico. Gareth made a great run from the left wing to get on the end of Dani Carvajal's cross. He was off the mark.

PLAY LIKE YOUR HEROES

GARETH BALE'S KNUCKLEBALL FREE-KICK

SEE IT HERE You Tube

https://www.youtube.com/watch?v=h0cYZcbxqbA

STEP 1: Win a free-kick in a goalscoring area.

STEP 2: Take a three-step run-up. Don't let the keeper know which side of the goal you're aiming for.

STEP 3: When you reach the ball, plant your supporting foot with your toes pointing towards the goal.

STEP 4: Make contact just below the centre of the ball with the front instep of your foot. You don't want to hit this free-kick right on the top of your laces.

STEP 5: Keep your body straight as you strike the ball. If you lean back, your shot will go high over the bar!

STEP 6: Don't follow-through after striking. Just stop and watch as the ball swerves past the keeper and into the net.

TEST YOUR KNOWLEDGE

QUESTIONS

1. Which football team did Gareth's Uncle Chris play for?

2. Who was Gareth's other childhood football hero?

3. When Gareth was scouted by Southampton Football Club aged eight, he moved to Southampton straight away. True or false?

4. Who was Gareth's best friend at Southampton?

5. How old was Gareth when he made his Southampton debut?

6. Gareth became Wales' youngest ever player. True or false?

7. How much did Tottenham pay to sign Gareth from Southampton?

8. Which Tottenham manager moved Gareth from left-back to left-wing?

9. When did Gareth start doing his heart goal celebration?

10. How many goals did Gareth score for Tottenham during the 2012-13 season?

11. Who was the Real Madrid manager when Gareth joined the club and what was the transfer fee?

Answers below. . . No cheating!

1. *Cardiff City* 2. *Ryan Giggs* 3. *False – Gareth trained at the club's Satellite Centre in Bath until he was sixteen* 4. *Theo Walcott* 5. *Sixteen* 6. *True – he was still only sixteen!* 7. *£5 million* 8. *Harry Redknapp* 9. 2010-11 season 10. 26 11. *Carlo Ancelotti was the manager and Gareth cost £85million.*

HAVE YOU GOT THEM ALL?

ULTIMATE FOOTBALL HEROES

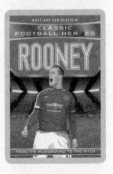